THE *DAILY EXPRESS*
FAMILY FOOD IN A FLASH

Beverley Piper is a freelance home economist who started writing about microwave cookery when working as a microwave oven demonstrator; she also presented a BBC series on microwave cookery. She originates recipes for various companies and often presents food for display, demonstrations and photography. Her previous books include *Super Juice* (1993), *The* Daily Express *Entertaining in a Flash* (1994) and *Super Juice for Slimmers* (1994), all published by Headline.

Beverley Piper is married to Malcolm Jarvis and they live in Kent.

GW00690618

The *Daily Express* Family Food in a Flash

Beverley Piper

Illustrations by
Mike Gordon

HEADLINE

First published in 1994
by HEADLINE BOOK PUBLISHING

10 9 8 7 6 5 4 3 2 1

ISBN 0 7472 4362 X

Typeset by
Letterpart Limited, Reigate, Surrey

Printed and bound in Great Britain by
Cox & Wyman Ltd, Reading, Berks.

HEADLINE BOOK PUBLISHING
A division of Hodder Headline PLC
338 Euston Road
London NW1 3BH

This book is dedicated to my husband,
Malcolm, with my love.

Contents

Acknowledgements

Grateful thanks to my secretary Tina Dorman who so carefully types the manuscript and also, on occasion, helps to test recipes.

Thanks to Adam Piper, Sam Jarvis and Rosie Watson for their help in testing the recipes speedily and accurately. Also, my grateful thanks to all my family and friends for their help and support and their continued enthusiasm in tasting many, many recipes.

Thanks to Billingtons for supplying sugar; Gordon Winterbottom at Hunter Saphir for supplying fruit and vegetables; Pilsbury marketing; Alison Jee at Vital PR and The National Dried Fruit Trade Association (UK) Ltd; to Wally Hollands at Beoco Ltd for supplying rape seed oil and to the Nestlé Company.

Author's Note

★ British standard measuring spoons, level, have been used throughout. These are available from most kitchen shops.
★ Recipes are given in both metric and imperial weights. Don't mix weights.
★ Where cartons, packets and tins are used, sizes printed on the actual products are used. Use the nearest size available.
★ Preparation times given are approximate and are timed from point where all ingredients and equipment have been assembled.

Introduction

Nowadays, most people catering for a family lead amazingly busy lives. There are so many different things to be done during the normal day that sometimes it seems nothing short of a miracle that we manage to feed the family at all!

This book is for you if you would like your family to be more healthy but you haven't got much time to cook. Healthy eating is really very easy. It needn't mean drastic changes – all you need is a little basic knowledge and recipes that are easy to follow. You'll find these aren't too expensive to put together, either. Don't think that giving your family healthy meals means that treats are taboo. Nobody has to cut out everything they enjoy. The important factor is to present a balanced diet and one that is so interesting and enjoyable that the family will prefer their new eating regime. There is room in the healthy diet for a few treats, so don't deny the family sweets and puddings completely. Just be aware of which foods are good and which foods should be treated as occasional indulgences.

As you flick through the following recipes you'll notice that reduced fat products have been used frequently, such as reduced calorie mayonnaise and reduced fat cream cheeses. Yoghurt and fromage frais feature fairly often too, and polyunsaturated fats and oils are often used instead of animal fats. High fibre wholemeal bread and brown rice are suggested as a change from white. The idea is that gradually you will enjoy a more healthy diet. Hopefully you'll be spoilt for choice – there are lots of quick and easy recipes with something for everyone.

BASIC HEALTHY EATING RULES FOR THE FAMILY

1. Cut out a few calories – excess weight is a major factor in high blood pressure, heart disease and many other

illnesses; it also spoils your looks and makes you lethargic and depressed.

2. Eat more fibre – fibre makes for a better diet with much more flavour, and fills you up too. Fibre is found in wholemeal bread, rice and pasta, breakfast cereals, fruit and vegetables.

3. Reduce your intake of fats – both animal and vegetable fats are frighteningly high in calories so cut down on fats both in cooking and spreading. Offer the family a low-fat spread alternative for bread and toast.

4. Cut down on sugar – sugar is a comfort food that leads to obesity and tooth decay. Make do with less – eat fresh and

dried fruits instead of sweets and biscuits etc.

5. Cut down on salt – salt is present in every manufactured food we eat, so although we need a little in the diet it is highly unlikely that you're not getting enough. Stop adding salt to cooking and leave it off the dining room table.

6. Don't be too rigid – just think along these lines for you and your family.

USING THIS BOOK

The book has been divided into two main parts. The first section is designed like any conventional cook book and is divided into chapters for quick and easy family cooking. There are plenty of starters, both hot and cold, and many can be assembled from storecupboard ingredients. The snack section is ideal for the busy household. Try Creamy Welsh Rarebit on page 55 for a speedy Saturday lunch or how about Pork Pittas on page 61 after football. There are over 20 main courses with something for everyone from Ratatouille with Haddock on page 118 to Sausage and Bramley Plait on page 108. Serving suggestions are given for each main meal so that you don't have to worry about choosing accompaniments.

The salad and vegetable dishes give colourful interesting recipes, some of which can be served as main meals. The Warm Potato Salad with Lemon and Sardines on page 73 is always popular in our house and the Tomato and Rice Salad on page 80 makes a great standby for entertaining.

The chapter on kids in the kitchen aims to encourage children to become involved in preparing food. With less and less cookery being taught in schools, there is a definite need for the next generation to learn something about food values and food preparation as they grow up. Spicy Beans with Frankfurters on page 159 is a simple recipe to start them off with, and I'm sure they'll love helping to make the Speedy Citrus Sponge Pud on page 176. As it's cooked to perfection in the microwave, they can enjoy seeing it rise before their very eyes!

The desserts chapter offers a wide range of puddings, some hot and some cold with several having a healthy fruity theme. Try the Blackcurrant Crumble on page 141 with a can of dairy custard for ease and speed, or the Blackcurrant and Redcurrant Fool on page 131 which is equally good made with fresh or frozen fruits. The Naughty but Nice chapter is exactly what it says – a bit of sheer indulgence. A little of what you fancy does occasionally do you good, so enjoy preparing Tiramisu for the family – there's a very easy recipe for this creamy Italian sweet that everyone adores on page 190 and just try and stop the kids eating the Mars Bar Flan on page 192!

The second part of the book includes eleven specially selected menus. Each has its own helpful time plan and is designed for a specific family occasion for varying numbers of people. Compiled to take the headache and worry from family parties, you're sure to find this section useful and will come back to the menus time and time again.

HINTS AND TIPS

1. As a basic rule, always serve more carbohydrate foods like rice, pasta, bread, with plenty of fruit and veg, less protein (cheese, eggs, fish, meat) and little fat and sugar. Your family will then be following a healthy diet naturally, they won't feel hungry and they'll be getting plenty of vitamins and minerals from their diet.
2. Assemble ingredients before starting any recipe so the task is quicker and far less stressful.
3. Wash up as you go along so you don't leave yourself with a sinkful of washing up after the meal. Fill used pans and dishes with cold water and set aside as soon as you've used them. You'll be surprised how much easier they are to wash up later.
4. Make good use of labour-saving equipment such as food processors and microwave ovens. The food processor is just like having another pair of hands in the kitchen. When you use it, ensure you prepare dry ingredients first – chop vegetables, slice potatoes, make breadcrumbs or

grate cheese for example, then purée or blend ingredients last. In this way you'll only have to wash the machine once, at the end.

5. Make more of your loaf – bread is a wonderful staple and many supermarkets now have a fresh bakery offering a vast selection of breads. Serve fresh bread, particularly wholemeal, often.

6. The quickest way to remove fat from a cooked casserole or mince dish is to drop a few ice cubes into it. The fat will harden and cling to the ice cubes which can then be lifted out with a draining spoon.

7. Change to low-fat cooking methods for speed and ease – grilling, steaming, microwaving, baking and simmering are far healthier than frying and roasting. They're considerably less messy too.

8. For instant family puds, offer fresh fruit or a diet yoghurt or diet fromage frais.

9. Get organized and shop for basics weekly. Make good use of the storecupboard, fridge and freezer and ensure that you gradually build up a supply of healthy foods you are able to turn into family meals fast, such as cans of pulses, fresh and frozen veg, canned tuna and salmon, brown rice and wholemeal pasta, etc. Always have a bowl of fresh fruit available – seasonal fruits are not expensive and they're full of essential vitamins, minerals and fibre.

10. For healthier snacks, have plenty of fresh fruit in the house and raw vegetables such as carrots, celery and tomatoes. Dried fruits such as dates, dried apricots, sultanas, raisins, etc., are naturally very sweet and far better for you than sweets, cakes, biscuits, etc.

PART ONE

Starters

Bacon & Walnut Salad
Serves 4

Crisp salad tossed with grilled bacon, crisp croûtons and walnuts makes a quick and easy starter that's suitable for many occasions.

Preparation time: 15 mins
Cooking time: 10 mins

For the salad
2 Little Gem lettuces, leaves separated and torn into pieces
4 small radishes, sliced

100g (4oz) mangetout, topped, tailed and each one halved at an angle
1 box mustard and cress

For the dressing
45ml (3 tablespoons) olive oil
15ml (1 tablespoon) red wine vinegar

Salt and freshly ground black pepper

For the topping
4 back bacon rashers, rinded and chopped
30ml (2 tablespoons) olive oil

2 slices wholemeal bread, crusts removed
50g (2oz) walnut pieces

To garnish
30ml (2 tablespoons) freshly chopped parsley

1. Put the lettuce into a mixing bowl with the radishes, mangetout and the mustard and cress. Cover and chill in the fridge.
2. Prepare the dressing. Put all ingredients in a screw-top jar and shake well.
3. Heat a non-stick frying pan and sauté the bacon until fat runs and bacon crisps. Remove using a draining spoon and drain on absorbent kitchen paper. Keep warm.
4. Add oil to pan and heat. Cut the bread into 2.5cm (½ inch) cubes and stir-fry in the heated oil until golden on all sides. Add walnut pieces and stir-fry briefly, just to heat. Remove using draining spoon and blot dry on absorbent kitchen paper.
5. When ready to serve, shake dressing again and pour on to salad. Toss to coat. Divide salad between four side plates. Top with bacon, croûtons of fried bread and walnut pieces.
6. Serve immediately, sprinkled with the parsley.

Mechouia Salad

Serves 4

A quick, luxurious salad that is served often in Turkey, Greece and Tunisia. Easy to make in advance, serve with French bread as a starter for a special occasion.

Preparation time: 10 mins
Cooking time: 5–8 mins

1 Italian beef steak tomato
1 medium onion, sliced
1 green pepper, halved and
  seeded
1 red pepper, halved and
  seeded
15ml (1 tablespoon) capers
Grated rind and juice of 1
  lemon

Salt and freshly ground
  black pepper
30ml (2 tablespoons) olive
  oil
225g (8oz) peeled prawns,
  defrosted if frozen
1 egg, hard-boiled and
  quartered
30ml (2 tablespoons) freshly
  chopped parsley

1. Pre-heat the grill to medium hot.
2. Cut the tomato into small dice, discarding the seeds. Put it into a medium mixing bowl.
3. Arrange sliced onions on the grill pan with the halved peppers. Cook under the pre-heated grill until browned, turning onion slices and peppers half-way through cooking.
4. Cut peppers and onions into small pieces. Add to mixing bowl.
5. Add capers, lemon rind and juice and a seasoning of salt and pepper to the bowl.
6. Sprinkle with the olive oil, then toss to coat.
7. Divide mixture between four side plates. Add prawns and the hard-boiled eggs to each plate.
8. Serve sprinkled with the chopped parsley.

Brie Parcels
Serves 4–6

Delicious, crispy savouries which are best served hot or warm. Ideal for an unusual starter, and great on the buffet table too. Use Cambozola or Dolcelatte as an alternative to Brie cheese.

Preparation time: 10 mins
Cooking time: 15–20 mins

50g (2oz) butter
100g (4oz) Brie cheese,
  cubed
100g (4oz) seedless black
  grapes, halved

50g (2oz) chopped walnuts
1 × 275g (10oz) packet filo
  pastry, defrosted if frozen
30ml (2 tablespoons) grated
  Parmesan cheese

To serve
salad garnish   *lemon mayonnaise*

1. Pre-heat the oven to 200°C (400°F) gas mark 6.
2. In a small mixing bowl, melt the butter in the microwave (1–2 minutes on defrost setting).
3. In a large mixing bowl, combine the Brie cheese with the grapes and walnuts.

4. Lay two sheets of filo on top of one another on a work surface or chopping board. Brush all over with melted butter. Put 1 dessertspoon filling in centre. Gather up edges and pinch together to form a Dick Whittington-like bundle. Brush all over with melted butter. Sprinkle with Parmesan cheese. Keep the filo sheets covered with a damp tea towel until you are ready to use them to prevent them drying out.
5. Repeat until all filling and filo has been used. You should have six parcels.
6. Arrange on lightly greased baking tray and bake for 15–20 minutes, until golden.
7. Serve warm or cold with a salad garnish and a dressing of lemon mayonnaise.

Cheesy Tomatoes

Serves 6

Large juicy tomatoes filled with a soufflé-like mixture, then
baked until golden. A delicious family starter or lunchtime
snack.

Preparation time: 10 mins
Cooking time: 15–20 mins

6 large beef tomatoes
175g (5oz) creamy fromage
 frais
1 clove garlic, crushed
Salt and freshly ground
 black pepper

75g (3oz) mature Cheddar
 cheese
5ml (1 teaspoon) dried basil
 or dill
2 eggs, size 3, separated

To garnish
sprigs of coriander or parsley

To serve
wholemeal toast

1. Pre-heat the oven to 200°C (400°F) gas mark 6.
2. Slice tops off tomatoes and hollow out insides using a
   teaspoon. Discard seeds and core.
3. Place shells on a non-stick baking sheet (if necessary slice
   a little off each base so the tomatoes sit upright).
4. Turn fromage frais into large mixing bowl. Add garlic and
   a little salt and pepper. Stir in half the Cheddar cheese
   with the basil or dill. Add egg yolks. Stir well.
5. In a clean bowl, whisk egg whites until they form peaks.
   Fold into cheese mixture using a metal spoon.

6. Spoon filling into tomato shells. Sprinkle with remaining Cheddar cheese.
7. Bake for 15–20 minutes until golden. Serve immediately with a coriander or parsley garnish, accompanied by freshly made wholemeal toast.

Stuffed Mushrooms
with Salad
Serves 4

A tasty starter that's cooked under the grill for ease and speed. Serve warm with granary bread rolls. Either use a bottled French dressing for the salad, or make your own.

Preparation time: 10 mins
Cooking time: 8–12 mins

8 medium size mushrooms
30ml (2 tablespoons) olive
 oil
10ml (2 teaspoons) lemon
 juice
25g (1oz) butter
6 spring onions, trimmed
 and finely sliced

5ml (1 teaspoon) dried
 oregano
2.5ml (¹/₂ teaspoon) dried
 thyme
225g (8oz) reduced fat cream
 cheese
50g (2oz) cooked, sliced
 gammon, chopped

To serve
225g (8oz) packet mixed
 salad leaves

45ml (3 tablespoons) French
 dressing

1. Pre-heat the grill to medium hot. Carefully remove stalks from mushrooms and reserve
2. Place mushrooms on foil lined grill pan. Combine the oil and lemon juice and brush on both sides of the mushrooms.
3. Grill for 5–8 minutes, until tender, turning once and brushing with more lemon juice and oil.
4. Melt the butter in a frying pan. Chop the mushroom stalks and add to the pan with the spring onions and herbs. Saute for 3–4 minutes, until tender. Drain on absorbent kitchen paper.

5. Put cream cheese into mixing bowl. Beat with a wooden spoon until smooth. Gradually beat in onions and herbs. Fold in gammon.
6. Pile a spoonful of cream cheese mixture onto each mushroom, gill side up.
7. In a clean mixing bowl, toss salad leaves in French dressing. Divide between four side plates. Top each salad with two mushrooms and serve immediately.

Crispy Mushrooms with Blue Cheese Dressing
Serves 4

A popular restaurant starter which is very easy to prepare at home. Choose even-sized mushrooms and use the stalks in a soup or sauce.

Preparation time: 15 mins + 15 mins chilling time
Cooking time: 6 mins

For the blue cheese dressing
150ml (5 fl oz) soured cream
30ml (2 tablespoons) reduced calorie mayonnaise
75g (3oz) Danish blue cheese
5ml (1 teaspoon) chopped chives
Salt and freshly ground black pepper
A few drops lemon juice

350g (12oz) medium size button mushrooms
175–200g (6–7oz) fresh white breadcrumbs (approx. 7 slices bread)
30ml (2 tablespoons) freshly chopped parsley
Salt and freshly ground black pepper
1 egg, size 2, beaten
Rape seed or sunflower seed oil for deep frying

1. Make the dressing. Put the soured cream into a mixing bowl with the mayonnaise. Crumble in the blue cheese then beat with a wooden spoon until smooth. Fold in the chives, a seasoning of salt and pepper and lemon juice to taste. Turn into serving dish. Cover with cling film and chill until ready to serve.
2. Wipe the mushrooms clean then cut off the stalks.
3. Combine breadcrumbs and parsley in a large mixing bowl.

Add a seasoning of salt and pepper.

4. Pour the beaten egg into a shallow plate. Dip the mushrooms in the beaten egg, about six at a time, then in the breadcrumbs, pressing the breadcrumbs on well. Transfer prepared mushrooms to a dinner plate and chill in the fridge for at least 15 minutes.

5. Heat the oil in a deep fat fryer to 190°C (375°F). (The oil is hot enough when a cube of bread dropped into the oil rises and turns golden almost instantly.)

6. Deep fry the mushrooms, a few at a time, for approximately 75 seconds, or until starting to brown. Drain on absorbent kitchen paper.

7. Continue until all mushrooms have been fried once.

8. Put half the mushrooms back into the hot oil. They will crisp and brown very quickly. Drain on absorbent kitchen paper and serve immediately with the blue cheese dressing.

9. Repeat with remaining mushrooms.

Garlic Mushrooms

Serves 4 as an accompaniment or 6 as a starter

Good as a light supper or lunch, garlic mushrooms are ever popular. Quick, simple and everyone's favourite, serve with lots of crusty bread to mop up the juices. An excellent starter served in warmed ramekins.

Preparation time: 5 mins
Cooking time: 7 mins

225g (8oz) field mushrooms
225g (8oz) chestnut mushrooms
50g (2oz) butter
10ml (2 teaspoons) olive oil
3 cloves garlic, crushed

4 spring onions, chopped
45ml (3 tablespoons) freshly chopped parsley
Juice of 1/2 lemon
Freshly ground black pepper

1. Wipe mushrooms clean with a damp cloth.
2. Slice mushrooms thickly, leaving stalks intact.
3. Heat butter and oil together in a large frying pan, until butter is foaming. Add garlic and spring onions. Sauté for 1–2 minutes then tip in the mushrooms, all in one go.

4. Fry the mushrooms over a medium heat, stirring frequently, for about 5–7 minutes.
5. Sprinkle over the parsley and lemon juice, then season with a little black pepper.
6. Turn into warmed serving dish and serve immediately with the crusty bread.

Crunchy Potato Boats
Serves 4

These crispy potato skins are easy to make and simply delicious with the almost instant soured cream dip. Just be aware that the skins of the potatoes are fairly soft after microwaving, so take care when you scoop out the flesh.

Preparation time: 10 mins
Cooking time: 35 mins

4 baking potatoes, about 225g (8oz) each
Olive oil for brushing

Salt for sprinkling and freshly ground black pepper
Rape seed or sunflower seed oil for deep frying

For the dip
150ml (5 fl oz) sour cream

30ml (2 tablespoons) freshly chopped chives

1. Scrub the potatoes and dry with absorbent kitchen paper. Prick each potato twice with a fork, then brush all over with a little oil. Sprinkle with salt.
2. Arrange the potatoes in a ring on a dinner plate.
3. Microwave on 100%/FULL power for 20 minutes, turning each potato over once after 10 minutes.
4. Allow the potatoes to stand for 5 minutes then cut each in half lengthways and scoop out the flesh and use it in another recipe, leaving a wall of potato about 1 cm (½ inch) thick on the skin. Cut each half skin in half again lengthways.
5. Meanwhile, heat the oil in a deep fat fryer to 190°C (375°F). The oil is hot enough when a cube of bread dropped into the oil rises and turns golden brown almost instantly.
6. Deep fry the potato skins, a few at a time, for 1–2 minutes or until crisp and golden. Drain on absorbent kitchen paper.
7. As soon as skins are fried, sprinkle with a little salt and serve with the soured cream dip.
8. To make the dip, simply blend soured cream and chives together with a seasoning of salt and pepper.

Curried Egg Starter
Serves 4

A simple curried adaptation of good old egg mayonnaise, this is a super starter to serve for dinner parties as it can be prepared well in advance or at the last minute, whichever method suits you best. Serve with wholemeal bread. These eggs are also excellent on the buffet table.

Preparation time: 10 mins
Cooking time: 8 mins

4 eggs, size 3

For the curry mayonnaise
85ml (4 fl oz) reduced calorie mayonnaise
85ml (4 fl oz) fromage frais
5ml (1 teaspoon) vegetable purée
10ml (2 teaspoons) curry paste or 2.5ml (¹/₂ teaspoon) medium curry powder

15ml (1 tablespoon) mango chutney
2.5ml (¹/₂ teaspoon) lime or lemon juice
Salt and freshly ground black pepper
15–30ml (1–2 tablespoons) milk

To serve
2 Little Gem lettuces

brown bread and butter

1. Put the eggs into a pan and cover with cold water.
2. Bring to the boil then cover with a lid and simmer for 8 minutes.
3. Drain and plunge the eggs into cold water. Set aside for 10 minutes.
4. Meanwhile, prepare the dressing.
5. Turn the mayonnaise into a mixing bowl. Add the fromage frais, vegetable purée, curry paste or powder and the

mango chutney, chopping the mango fruit into small pieces first.

6. Stir to blend, then stir in the lime or lemon juice and a seasoning of salt and pepper to taste. Add milk to produce a coating sauce.

7. Divide the lettuce leaves between four side plates, shredding them if necessary. Shell and halve the eggs then arrange two halves of egg, yolk side down on each lettuce garnish.

8. Spoon over the curry mayonnaise to coat eggs evenly. Serve immediately.

Fanned Avocado with Crème de Fraises

Serves 4

Choose top quality avocados for this fruity flavoured starter and make sure they are perfectly ripe. Ripe avocados 'give' slightly when gently squeezed. Try to buy the avocados two or three days before you want to use them and ripen them off in a warm kitchen.

Preparation time: 10 mins
Cooking time: 0

2 large, ripe avocado pears
Juice of ½ lime

60ml (4 tablespoons) crème de fraises liqueur
2 strawberries

1. Halve the avocados and remove the stones. Carefully peel each half.
2. Lay each peeled avocado half, flat side down, on a board. Cut evenly across into slices, lengthways, without cutting right through the top thin end. 'Fan' the slices out gently. Sprinkle each fan with a little lime juice.
3. Pour 15ml (1 tablespoon) crème de fraises on each of four side plates to form a pool.
4. Lift an avocado fan carefully onto each side plate.
5. Cut each strawberry in half through stalk. Fan the strawberry halves, slicing slightly away from the stalk end. Place one strawberry fan on uncut end of each avocado fan. Serve immediately.

Tuna Briks

Serves 4

A favourite starter or snack meal in Tunisia, these crispy pastries should be served hot and eaten with the hands. The trick is not to end up with egg dripping down your chin! Serve with a salad garnish and a wedge of lemon.

Preparation time: 10 mins
Cooking time: 2–3 mins for each brik

*4 sheets filo pastry, defrosted
  if frozen
1 small onion, finely
  chopped
185g (6½oz) can tuna in oil,
  drained
15ml (1 tablespoon) freshly
  chopped parsley*

*Salt and freshly ground
  black pepper
4 eggs, size 3
Corn oil for shallow frying
  (you will need enough oil
  to be approx. 1.25cm (¼
  inch) deep in a frying pan)*

To serve
salad garnish   *wedges of lemon*

1. Lay one sheet of filo out on a dinner plate. Keep the other filo sheets covered with a damp tea towel until you are ready to use them, to prevent them drying out.
2. Put a quarter of the chopped onion into the centre. Add a quarter of the drained tuna and a quarter of the parsley. Season with a little salt and pepper.
3. Using the back of a teaspoon, make an indent in the filling mixture. Break an egg into this.
4. Fold in edges of filo, then fold over to form a large triangle. Seal edges by pressing together.
5. Heat the oil in a large, shallow frying pan until shimmering, then slide the brik from the plate into the hot oil.

6. Cook for 1–2 minutes, until puffed up and golden. Turn using two fish slices and cook second side for 1–2 minutes until golden.
7. Drain on absorbent kitchen paper and serve with the salad garnish and a wedge of lemon for squeezing over.
8. Repeat until all pastry and filling has been used and you have cooked four briks.

Mussels in Cider

Serves 4

Mussels are becoming increasingly popular as a starter or light lunch. They are readily available in supermarkets, raw or ready cooked and out of their shells.

Preparation time: 5 mins
Cooking time: 8 mins

250ml (8 fl oz) dry cider
15ml (1 tablespoon)
* wholegrain mustard*
Freshly ground black pepper

450g (1lb) cooked mussels,
* out of their shells*
15ml (1 tablespoon) freshly
* chopped parsley*
10ml (2 teaspoons) cornflour

To garnish
30ml (2 tablespoons) chopped parsley

1. Put the cider into a large saucepan with the mustard and a seasoning of black pepper. Bring to the boil.
2. Reduce heat to low and add the mussels. Cover with a lid and simmer gently for 3–4 minutes until mussels are piping hot.
3. Lift mussels onto a warmed serving dish, using a draining spoon. Reserve cooking liquid in the pan. Stir parsley into pan.
4. Blend the cornflour with 15ml (1 tablespoon) water in a cup, then stir into cooking liquid.
5. Heat, stirring, until sauce thickens slightly. Pour sauce over the mussels and serve immediately, garnished with the chopped parsley.

Salmon &
Lime Pâté

Serves 4–6

This creamy pâté is equally good served on the buffet table or as a starter for a special family meal. I often serve it for a quick lunch too, with some salad, chunky brown bread and tomato relish.

Preparation time: 10 mins
Cooking time: 0

175g (6oz) reduced fat cream cheese
Grated rind and juice of ¹/₂ lime
200g (7oz) can red salmon
10ml (2 teaspoons) tomato purée

60ml (4 tablespoons) crème fraîche or fromage frais
10ml (2 teaspoons) dried tarragon
Salt and freshly ground black pepper

To garnish
twists of lime

To serve
wholemeal toast

1. Put cream cheese into food processor with the rind and juice from the lime. Add the liquid from the salmon, then discard bones and skin of the fish and flake flesh into food processor. Process until smooth.
2. Add tomato purée, crème fraîche or fromage frais and tarragon with a seasoning of salt and pepper. Process just to combine.

3. Turn mixture into suitable dish and chill until ready to serve.
4. Serve the pâté garnished with the twists of lime and accompanied by the wholemeal toast.

Fishy Sambal
Serves 4

Serve this fishy relish as a starter or appetizer dip with
pre-dinner drinks. Good served on canapés, too, or with slices
of cucumber as part of a buffet table.

Note: The whipping cream will thicken as you whizz ingredients into the machine, so be careful not to over-process.

Preparation time: 15 mins
Cooking time: 0

198g (7oz) can tuna in oil,
   drained
250ml (8 fl oz) carton
   whipping cream
1 shallot, chopped
1 clove garlic, chopped
2.5ml (1/2 teaspoon) chilli
   powder (or to taste)

5ml (1 teaspoon) anchovy
   essence
5ml (1 teaspoon) ground
   coriander
10ml (2 teaspoons) tomato
   purée
Salt

To serve
fresh vegetable sticks   *small crackers*

1. Flake the tuna into the food processor.
2. Add the cream, shallot, garlic and chilli powder. Process for a few seconds, until smooth.
3. Add the anchovy essence, coriander and tomato purée. Process again until smooth.
4. Transfer to suitable bowl. Serve immediately or chill until ready to serve.

Chicken Satay

Serves 4

Serve these tasty kebabs with the quick satay dipping sauce on page 36 garnished with a few chopped peanuts. A delicious, popular starter, accompany with a mixed salad garnish. You will need 8 wooden skewers, soaked in cold water for at least 10 minutes before using.

Preparation time: 10 mins + marinating time
Cooking time: 8–10 mins

450g (1lb) chicken breast fillet
2 spring onions, peeled and finely chopped
45ml (3 tablespoons) dark soy sauce

5ml (1 teaspoon) dark muscovado sugar
10ml (2 teaspoons) rape seed oil
Finely grated rind of 1 lemon
15ml (1 tablespoon) freshly chopped coriander

To serve
salad garnish

1. Cut the chicken into 1cm (½ inch) dice.
2. In a shallow dish mix together the spring onions, soy sauce, sugar, oil, lemon rind and coriander. Add the chicken. Toss until coated with the marinade mixture then cover and set aside, at room temperature, for 15 minutes or up to 2 hours in the fridge (whichever is more convenient).
3. When ready to serve, pre-heat the grill to hot.
4. Thread the chicken cubes on to the 8 skewers, pushing them fairly close together.
5. Grill the kebabs for 4–5 minutes each side, until well browned and tender. Serve immediately.

Satay Dipping Sauce
Serves 4

Serve this spicy cold dip with chicken or pork satay, or just
with crisps and vegetable sticks. Quick to prepare and very
tasty!

Preparation time: 5 mins
Cooking time: 0

*60ml (4 tablespoons)
  crunchy peanut butter*
*5ml (1 teaspoon) dark soy
  sauce*

*1.25ml ($^1/_4$ teaspoon) chilli
  powder (or to taste)*
*1 small clove garlic
  (optional)*
200ml (7 fl oz) crème fraîche

To serve
selection of vegetable sticks, bread sticks and crisps

1. Put peanut butter into food processor. Add soy sauce,
   chilli powder, garlic and crème fraîche.
2. Process until smooth. It may be necessary to stop the
   machine and scrape ingredients from sides with a spatula
   once or twice.
3. Turn into suitable dish, then cover and refrigerate until
   ready to serve.

Curried Mango Dip
Serves 4–6

A dip that's almost instant to prepare, isn't too high on calories and tastes simply wonderful. Serve with apples, pineapple, celery, and red and green peppers.

Preparation time: 10 mins
Cooking time: 0

30ml (2 tablespoons) reduced fat mayonnaise

5ml (1 teaspoon) mild curry powder

30ml (2 tablespoons) mango chutney

200ml (7 fl oz) carton crème fraîche

30ml (2 tablespoons) freshly chopped spring onions

Salt

To serve
1 green-skinned eating apple
1 red-skinned eating apple
Juice of 1/2 lemon
3 canned pineapple rings, drained

2 sticks celery
1/2 red pepper
1/2 green pepper

1. Put the mayonnaise into a mixing bowl. Add the curry powder, chutney (chop the pieces of mango first) and crème fraîche.
2. Mix well then stir in the spring onions and season to taste with a little salt. Turn into suitable serving dish and chill until ready to serve.
3. Core and slice the apples and sprinkle with the lemon juice. Cut the pineapple rings into cubes. Cut the celery into large matchsticks and cut the red and green peppers into strips, discarding seeds.
4. Serve the dip surrounded by the vegetables and fruits.

Soured Cream & Coriander Dip
Serves 4

A fresh-tasting dip which is excellent served with tortilla chips and vegetable sticks.

Preparation time: 5 mins
Cooking time: 0

150ml (5 fl oz) soured
  cream, chilled
30ml (2 tablespoons) ground
  hazelnuts
45ml (3 tablespoons) freshly
  chopped coriander

10ml (2 teaspoons)
  concentrated mint sauce
2.5ml (1/2 teaspoon) lime
  juice
Salt and pinch cayenne
  pepper

To serve
tortilla chips

celery, red pepper and
  carrots, cut into fingers

1. Put the soured cream into a mixing bowl. Add hazelnuts, coriander, mint sauce and lime juice. Stir to blend.
2. Season to taste with the salt and cayenne. Turn into serving dish and serve immediately with the tortilla chips and vegetable sticks, or cover with cling film and chill in the fridge until ready to serve.

Easy Mushroom Soup
Serves 4–6

This simple soup tastes wonderfully creamy and full of flavour. Great on Bonfire Night and Hallowe'en or as a starter before almost any main course. Serve with warm bread rolls.

Preparation time: 10 mins
Cooking time: 23 mins

*50g (2oz) butter or
  polyunsaturated margarine*
*225g (8oz) mushrooms,
  finely chopped*
*1 medium onion, peeled and
  finely chopped*
40g (1¹/₂oz) plain flour

*600ml (1 pint) chicken or
  vegetable stock*
*300ml (10 fl oz)
  semi-skimmed milk*
*Salt and freshly ground
  black pepper*

To serve
*60ml (4 tablespoons)
  whipping cream*

*30ml (2 tablespoons) freshly
  chopped parsley*

1. In a large saucepan melt the butter or margarine. When foaming, add mushrooms and onion and sauté for 5 minutes until softened.
2. Add the flour and cook, stirring, for 1 minute.
3. Gradually stir in the stock. Bring to a rapid boil, stirring continuously, then cover and simmer for 15 minutes, stirring occasionally.
4. Stir in milk and season lightly to taste. Return to boil, stirring. Simmer for 2 minutes.
5. Serve the soup in soup bowls, topping each serving with a spoonful of cream and a sprinkling of parsley.

Chinese Broth

Serves 4

This Chinese-flavoured soup is a good way to use up the end of a roast chicken. Serve as a starter with bread rolls or with cheese scones as a quick lunch.

Preparation time: 10 mins
Cooking time: 16 mins

1 medium onion, finely chopped
1 clove garlic, crushed
1 leek, washed and sliced
175g (6oz) potatoes, peeled and diced
6 large button mushrooms, halved and sliced
100g (4oz) broccoli spears
100g (4oz) frozen peas

400g (14oz) can chopped tomatoes
75g (3oz) frozen sweetcorn kernels
900ml (1¹/₂ pints) beef stock
5ml (1 teaspoon) dried oregano
175g (6oz) cold cooked chicken, chopped
Salt and freshly ground black pepper

1. Put onion and garlic into a cereal bowl. Cover with a side plate and microwave for 2 minutes on 100%/FULL power.
2. Put onion, garlic, leek, potatoes, mushrooms, broccoli, peas, tomatoes and sweetcorn into a large saucepan.
3. Pour over the beef stock then add the oregano. Bring to the boil, cover the pan and simmer for 10 minutes. Add chicken. Continue to simmer for 3–4 minutes.
4. Season to taste with a little salt and pepper then serve immediately.

French Onion Soup
Serves 4

A traditional French soup that's quick and easy to prepare. With its topping of bread and melted cheese, this recipe is ideal for a quick lunch or supper.

Note: For ease, stand soup bowls on side plates when you grill the bread and cheese and use oven gloves to remove them.

Preparation time: 10 mins
Cooking time: 25 mins

25g (1oz) butter
15ml (1 tablespoon) rape seed oil
4 medium onions, sliced
30ml (2 tablespoons) plain flour
1 litre (1¾ pints) beef stock
5ml (1 teaspoon) dried oregano

Salt and freshly ground black pepper
45ml (3 tablespoons) medium dry sherry
8 slices from a French loaf
100g (4oz) Gruyère cheese, grated

1. Heat butter and oil in a large saucepan until butter melts. Add onions and sauté for 10–12 minutes until softened and lightly golden.
2. Add flour and cook, stirring, for 1 minute.
3. Gradually add stock, stirring. Bring to the boil, then add oregano and season with a little salt and pepper.
4. Cover and simmer for 10 minutes. Add sherry, then continue to simmer for 5 minutes.
5. Pour soup into four soup bowls. Float two slices of bread on top of each bowl of soup. Sprinkle with cheese.
6. Pop under a hot grill for a few minutes until cheese melts and bubbles.
7. Serve immediately.

Carrot & Tomato Soup
Serves 4

A warming soup that's high on flavour yet low on calories.
Serve with French bread.

Preparation time: 15 mins
Cooking time: 30 mins

10ml (2 teaspoons) olive oil
25g (1oz) lean streaky
   bacon, chopped
1 medium onion, chopped
225g (8oz) carrots, diced
Rind and juice of ½ orange
400g (14oz) can peeled plum
   tomatoes

15ml (1 tablespoon) tomato
   purée
5ml (1 teaspoon) dried basil
600ml (1 pint) chicken stock
Salt and freshly ground
   black pepper

To serve
70g (2¾oz) packet herb and garlic flavoured croûtons
   (optional)

1. In a medium size non-stick saucepan, heat the oil. Sauté
   the bacon with the onion for about 5 minutes, until onion
   softens.
2. Add carrots and continue to sauté for 1–2 minutes.
3. Add all remaining ingredients. Season with a little salt and
   pepper. Chop tomatoes roughly in the pan.
4. Bring to the boil, stirring occasionally. Cover with a lid
   and simmer for 20 minutes.
5. Transfer to food processor and process until smooth.
6. Return to pan and re-heat gently to serve.
7. Serve in warmed soup bowls, sprinkled with the croûtons.

Snacks

Vegetable Broth
Serves 4

For a quick and easy lunchtime snack this soup is ideal. Low in calories and suitable for vegetarians, try it with chunks of wholemeal bread or warm baguettes.

Preparation time: 15 mins
Cooking time: 25 mins

2 carrots, sliced
100g (4oz) swede, diced into small dice
100g (4oz) mushrooms, sliced

1 medium size courgette, sliced
225g (8oz) potatoes, diced
1 litre (1³/4 pints) vegetable stock
50g (2oz) frozen peas

1. Place carrots, swede, mushrooms, courgette, potatoes and stock in a medium size pan.
2. Bring to the boil, cover with a lid and simmer for 20 minutes. Add peas and return to simmer, covered for a further 5 minutes.
3. Serve immediately.

Seafood Spaghetti
Serves 4

Families love spaghetti and this seafood version is very quick to prepare and fairly inexpensive. A delicious starter or lunchtime snack for four. Serve with French bread.

Preparation time: 5 mins
Cooking time: 14 mins

25g (1oz) butter
2 leeks, cleaned and sliced thinly
1 clove garlic, crushed (optional)
450g (1lb) spaghetti
5ml (1 teaspoon) oil
200ml (7 fl oz) dry cider
150ml (5 fl oz) double cream

Salt and freshly ground black pepper
198g (7oz) can tuna in oil, drained and flaked
100g (4oz) peeled prawns, defrosted if frozen
100g (4oz) frozen peas, defrosted

To serve
freshly chopped parsley

1. Heat the butter in a large saucepan until foaming. Add the leeks and garlic. Sauté for 5–7 minutes until softened.
2. Cook the spaghetti in a large pan of boiling salted water with the oil for 8–10 minutes until *al dente* (tender but still retaining a bite) or as directed on packet.
3. Meanwhile, add the cider, cream and a seasoning of salt and pepper to the leeks. Bring to the boil and simmer for a few minutes to reduce slightly. Add tuna, prawns and peas to the sauce. Cook, stirring, for 2–3 minutes.
4. Drain the spaghetti, toss with the seafood sauce until well mixed then serve immediately garnished with plenty of chopped parsley.

Cheesy Champ
Serves 4

Champ is one of Ireland's most traditional potato dishes. This version adds Swiss Gruyère cheese to make a delicious quick supper or lunch. Serve with a simple mixed salad.

Note: If you have a little more time, turn the cheesy potato into a greased pie dish and top with an extra 25g (1oz) of grated cheese. Pop under a pre-heated grill until cheese melts and bubbles.

Preparation time: 15 mins
Cooking time: 13 mins

750g (1lb 12oz) old potatoes, peeled and cut into fairly large dice
Salt and freshly ground black pepper
150ml (5 fl oz) semi-skimmed milk

1 bunch spring onions, chopped finely
25g (1oz) butter or low-fat spread
100g (4oz) Gruyère or mature Cheddar cheese, grated

To serve
mixed salad

1. Put the potatoes into a large microwavable bowl. Add a seasoning of salt and pepper.
2. Pour over the milk.
3. Cover and microwave on 100%/FULL power for approximately 13 minutes. Allow to stand, covered for 5 minutes.
4. Mash potatoes well, then beat until fluffy with a wooden spoon.
5. Fold in spring onions, butter and cheese to melt. Serve immediately with a salad garnish.

Sausagy Peppers

Serves 4

Colourful bell peppers combined with sausagemeat flavoured with garlic and parsley make delicious snacks or starters which are great for the family. They are also good cut in half again and served warm on the buffet table.

Preparation time: 15 mins
Cooking time: 20 mins

2 red peppers
2 green peppers
50g (2oz) freshly made
brown breadcrumbs
225g (8oz) pork
sausagemeat, reduced fat
variety if preferred

30ml (2 tablespoons) freshly
chopped parsley
3 spring onions, chopped
2 cloves garlic, crushed
Salt and freshly ground
black pepper
25g (1oz) grated Cheddar
cheese

To serve
15ml (1 tablespoon) freshly chopped parsley

1. Pre-heat the oven to 200°C (400°F) gas mark 6.
2. Wash and dry the peppers and cut each one in half lengthwise. Remove core and seeds.
3. Arrange skin side down on a lightly greased baking sheet and bake in the pre-heated oven for 10 minutes. Remove and set aside to cool.
4. In a large mixing bowl, mix the breadcrumbs into the sausagemeat. Add the parsley, onions and garlic (this is easiest done with clean hands or in a food processor). Season with a little salt and pepper.

5. Use the mixture to stuff each pepper half. Sprinkle with the grated cheese.
6. Bake for 20 minutes. Serve warm or cold, sprinkled with the freshly chopped parsley.

Grilled Corn on the Cob
Serves 4

Mini frozen cobs of corn are a convenient, healthy snack to keep in the freezer. Kids love them and will enjoy this grilled version even more.

Preparation time: 5 mins
Cooking time: 13 mins

8 mini corn on the cobs

50g (2oz) melted butter to serve or 30ml (2 tablespoons) Pura Light Touch

1. Cook corn cobs in lightly salted water for 6 minutes. Drain.
2. Meanwhile, pre-heat the grill to medium hot.
3. Brush cobs with melted butter or Pura, then grill under the pre-heated grill for 5–7 minutes turning frequently, until lightly golden.
4. Serve immediately with the remaining butter or Pura poured over.

Edam, Mushroom
& Tomato Kebabs
Serves 4

These tasty kebabs may be cooked on the barbecue or under the grill. Wonderful served warm at the point when the cheese just starts to melt.

Note: If using wooden kebab sticks, make sure you soak them in water for at least 10 minutes before using to prevent them burning.

Preparation time: 10 mins
Cooking time: 5 mins

For the glaze
1 clove garlic, crushed
Juice of 1 lime
30ml (2 tablespoons) freshly snipped basil and parsley

30ml (2 tablespoons) olive oil
Salt and freshly ground black pepper

225g (8oz) mini Edam cheeses
4 thick slices from a wholemeal French loaf, cubed

8 Italian tomatoes, halved
8 button mushrooms

To serve
mixed salad

black and green olives, stoned

1. Pre-heat the grill or barbecue.
2. Prepare the glaze. Combine all ingredients for the glaze in a small mixing bowl and whisk with a fork.
3. Remove the rind from the cheeses. Thread the cubed

bread, halved tomatoes, mushrooms and cheese on to the four kebab sticks.

4. Brush the kebabs all over with the glaze, allowing the bread to soak up the glaze.

5. Grill or barbecue the kebabs for about 2 minutes each side, until the bread crisps and the cheese starts to melt.

6. Serve immediately with the salad garnish and the olives.

Grapefruit &
Chicken Mayonnaise
Serves 4

Serve with chunks of French bread, this healthy snack is a good way to use up leftover chicken.

Preparation time: 10 mins
Cooking time: 0

1 pink grapefruit, peeled
1 red-skinned crisp eating apple, cored and chopped
175g (6oz) cooked chicken, chopped roughly

Salt and freshly ground black pepper
100g (4oz) seedless green grapes
3 Iceberg lettuce leaves, shredded

For the dressing
30ml (2 tablespoons) reduced calorie mayonnaise
5ml (1 teaspoon) mild curry powder

Pinch ground coriander
10ml (2 teaspoons) apricot jam
150ml (5 fl oz) low-fat fromage frais

To serve
sprinkling of paprika

1. Segment the grapefruit, discarding membrane and reserving any juice. Cut each segment into three and put into a mixing bowl.
2. Add apple, chicken, a seasoning of salt and pepper and the grapes.
3. In a separate mixing bowl, beat together the mayonnaise, curry powder, coriander, apricot jam and fromage frais. Stir any reserved grapefruit juice into the dressing.

4. Pour dressing over fruit and chicken mixture. Toss to coat.
5. Arrange shredded lettuce on four side plates. Top with chicken mixture and sprinkle with paprika.
6. Serve immediately.

Fruity Snack
Serves 4

Many people prefer a bowl of high fibre, interesting fruits as a snack instead of a sandwich. This recipe has plenty of fibre and vitamins and can be put together quickly at most times of the year.

Preparation time: 10 mins
Cooking time: 0

1 Ogen melon
100g (4oz) seedless black
* grapes*
1 ripe pear
1 eating apple

1 banana
120ml (4 fl oz) apple juice
225g (8oz) Greek yoghurt
25g (1oz) honey-roasted
* sunflower seeds*

1. Cut melon in half. Remove seeds then peel and dice flesh, reserving any juice. Put into a mixing bowl. Add grapes.
2. Core and dice pear and apple and add to bowl.
3. Peel and slice banana and add to bowl. Pour over apple juice. Toss to coat.
4. Divide fruit between four sundae dishes. Top each fruit salad with a spoonful of Greek yoghurt and sprinkle with sunflower seeds before serving.

Creamy Welsh Rarebit
Serves 4

A very quick way to make a creamy Welsh rarebit. Serve with a salad garnish as a snack lunch or for children's tea.

Preparation time: 10 mins
Cooking time: 5–7 mins

*4 slices wholemeal bread
  from a thick sliced cut loaf
175g (6oz) Edam cheese,
  grated
30ml (2 tablespoons)
  reduced calorie
  mayonnaise*

*30ml (2 tablespoons)
  fromage frais
Salt and freshly ground
  black pepper*

To serve
salad garnish

1. Toast both sides of the bread lightly.
2. Put cheese into a mixing bowl and add mayonnaise and fromage frais. Season with salt and pepper. Stir to mix well.
3. Spread cheese mixture evenly over toast.
4. Grill until bubbling and golden. Serve immediately with the salad garnish.

Pastrami & Fruit Danish Sandwiches
Serves 4

Spoil the family with this sophisticated snack. Great for teenagers who want to impress their friends.

Preparation time: 10 mins
Cooking time: 0

1 large orange, peeled
4 slices rye crispbread
Butter or low-fat spread

4 thin slices Pastrami
Salad leaves

1. Segment the orange, discarding pith and membrane.
2. Spread crispbread with butter or low-fat spread.
3. Arrange orange segments and pastrami attractively on crispbreads.
4. Garnish with salad leaves and serve immediately.

Spicy Baps

Serves 4

Mayonnaise with chutney and Cheddar, lightly toasted under the grill, makes a particularly tasty teatime treat that's so welcome on a cold winter's evening. Also delicious served cold, so could be added to the lunch box too.

Preparation time: 10 mins
Cooking time: 5 mins

4 bap rolls
60ml (4 tablespoons) tomato chutney or sweet pickle
60ml (4 tablespoons) reduced calorie mayonnaise

100g (4oz) Cheddar cheese, grated
1 Cox's apple, cored and sliced

To serve
sticks of celery
tomatoes

1. Pre-heat the grill to medium heat.
2. Split each bap into two halves.
3. Combine chutney and mayonnaise in a mixing bowl and spread onto the baps.
4. Top evenly with the grated cheese. Grill under the pre-heated grill until lightly golden. Top with the sliced apple and serve with the celery and tomatoes.

Chicken Tikka
French Stick

Serves 4

The tikka filling is delicious with coriander bread in this substantial snack. Prepare the French stick as you would garlic bread.

Preparation time: 15 mins
Cooking time: 10 mins

Approx. 50g (2oz) butter or low-fat spread
15ml (1 tablespoon) freshly chopped coriander

1 French stick, cut into four even pieces, vertically

For the filling
60ml (4 tablespoons) reduced calorie mayonnaise
150ml (5 fl oz) plain yoghurt
15ml (1 tablespoon) lemon juice
10ml (2 teaspoons) paprika pepper

5ml (1 teaspoon) mild chilli powder
1 clove garlic, crushed
Salt
50g (2oz) sultanas
5cm (2 inch) piece cucumber, diced
450g (1lb) cooked chicken breast, diced

To serve
mixed salad

1. Pre-heat oven to 200°C (400°F) gas mark 6.
2. Beat together butter and coriander. Slit each quarter of the French stick all along length, at 2.5cm (1 inch) intervals, without cutting right through. Spread cuts with butter. Sandwich together and wrap each piece

loosely in foil. Stand on two baking sheets and bake for 10 minutes.

3. Meanwhile prepare the filling. Put mayonnaise into a mixing bowl. Beat in yoghurt, lemon juice, paprika, chilli powder, garlic and salt to blend, using a wooden spoon. Fold in sultanas, cucumber and chicken until coated with dressing.

4. Serve one piece of hot French stick per person with a quarter of the chicken tikka filling. Each person can pull off portions of the hot bread and eat it with the filling.

Banana & Peanut Butter Club Sandwich

Serves 4

Kids will love these tiered sandwiches. Good for a nutritious and filling lunchtime snack, or try serving them in the evening with a hot drink.

Preparation time: 15 mins
Cooking time: 5 mins

225g (8oz) back bacon
8 slices wholemeal bread
30–45ml (2–3 tablespoons)
 peanut butter
45ml (3 tablespoons)
 reduced calorie
 mayonnaise

45ml (3 tablespoons)
 fromage frais
4 slices multigrain bread
1 Little Gem lettuce
1 banana, sliced

1. Grill bacon until crisp, then chop roughly.
2. Spread four wholemeal bread slices with peanut butter.
3. Top with the chopped bacon.
4. Mix the mayonnaise and fromage frais together. Spread both sides of multigrain bread with mayonnaise mixture and put on top of bacon. Top with lettuce and sliced banana.
5. Spread rest of mayonnaise mixture on one side of the remaining four slices of wholemeal bread and place on top, mayonnaise side down. Press sandwiches firmly together.
6. Cut each sandwich into four triangles and secure with cocktail sticks. Serve immediately.

Pork Pittas

Serves 4

Pitta pockets, warmed under the grill, then filled with a speedy, tasty meat sauce and salad makes a quick lunch or supper that's hearty enough for most appetites. The chillies are added as my family love mince with a bit of a kick – use enough to suit your taste!

Preparation time: 10 mins
Cooking time: 28 mins

15ml (1 tablespoon) corn oil
1 medium onion, chopped
2 rashers streaky bacon, rinded and chopped
1.25–2.5ml (1/4–1/2 teaspoon) dried chopped chillies
350g (12oz) lean minced pork

100g (4oz) button mushrooms, chopped
385g (13 1/2oz) can red wine and tomato sauce (supermarkets' own label are excellent)
4 pitta breads

For the salad
Approx. 175g (6oz) Iceberg lettuce, shredded
1/2 medium onion, finely sliced

5cm (2 inch) piece cucumber, diced

1. Prepare the meat sauce. In a medium size saucepan, heat the oil then fry the onion and bacon for 5 minutes, stirring frequently. Stir in dried chillies with the pork and mushrooms and continue to fry, stirring, for 3–4 minutes to seal the meat.
2. Add the can of sauce, stir well. Gradually bring to the boil. Cover with a lid and simmer for 20 minutes, stirring once or twice.

3. When ready to serve, heat the pitta breads briefly under the grill. Split pittas open.
4. Divide meat sauce between pittas. Top with the salad ingredients and serve immediately.

Savoury Cheese Loaf
Serves 4

A popular snack which is easy to prepare and quick to bake. Ideal for a speedy lunch or supper. Serve either with a bowl of soup or with a tossed mixed salad. For variations to this recipe, try a slice of lean ham with each slice of cheese or use sweet pickle with the cheese instead of mustard.

Preparation time: 10 mins
Cooking time: 15–20 mins

1 small bloomer loaf
Low-fat spread for spreading
15ml (1 tablespoon) Dijon
  mustard

8 Cheddar cheese slices,
  halved into triangles
3 tomatoes, sliced
Salt and freshly ground
  black pepper

1. Pre-heat the oven to 240°C (475°F) gas mark 9.
2. Make 10 even cuts through the loaf, as though you were going to make garlic bread, so don't cut right through base.
3. Spread both sides of each cut slice of bread with a little low-fat spread and then with a little mustard.
4. Put 1 or 2 cheese triangles into each section.
5. Add 2 tomato slices to each section, season with salt and pepper, then wrap the loaf completely in a large sheet of foil.
6. Bake for 15–20 minutes, until cheese melts. Serve immediately.

Carrot, Banana & Walnut Cake

Makes 12 slices

Even if you haven't had much success with microwave cakes in the past, do try this one as it cooks brilliantly and provides a substantial snack that's high in fibre. The creamy filling isn't absolutely necessary but it does make the cake special. You will need a 23cm (9 in) round cake pan, suitable for microwave ovens, or a 1.4 litre (2½ pint) loaf pan.

Preparation time: 10–15 mins
Cooking time: 7–10 mins

225g (8oz) wholemeal self-raising flour
75g (3oz) muscovado dark brown sugar
175g (6oz) carrot, finely grated
1 medium ripe banana, mashed

2 eggs, size 2, beaten
60ml (4 tablespoons) sunflower oil
150ml (5 fl oz) orange juice
Grated rind of ½ orange
50g (2oz) walnuts, chopped

For the filling
100g (4oz) reduced fat cream cheese
25g (1oz) sifted icing sugar

10ml (2 teaspoons) lemon juice
Grated rind of ½ lemon

To serve
a little sifted icing sugar

1. Put the flour, sugar, carrot, banana, eggs, oil, orange juice and rind into a mixing bowl.
2. Beat with a wooden spoon or electric mixer until well mixed. Stir in the walnuts.

3. Turn into lightly greased and base lined cake pan.
4. Microwave on 100%/FULL power for 7–10 minutes or until a wooden cocktail stick inserted in centre comes out clean. Leave to stand for 10 minutes.
5. Cool on wire rack.
6. When cold, split cake in half.
7. Prepare the filling. Put all ingredients for the filling into a mixing bowl and beat to combine.
8. Sandwich cake with filling mixture then arrange on serving dish.
9. Serve topped with a little sifted icing sugar.

Salads &
Vegetable Dishes

Salade Niçoise

Serves 4 or 6 as a starter

This ever popular salad is quick and easy to prepare. It serves 4 as an accompaniment, makes an excellent starter for 6 or a buffet party addition. You may like to hand a bowl of reduced calorie mayonnaise round separately.

Preparation time: 10 mins
Cooking time: 0

225g (8oz) French beans, fresh or frozen
225g (8oz) cherry tomatoes, halved
4 spring onions, chopped
1 Little Gem lettuce
2 sticks celery, chopped finely
$\frac{1}{2}$ green pepper, seeded and thinly sliced

85ml (3 fl oz) reduced fat French dressing
198g (7oz) can tuna in brine, drained and flaked
50g (2oz) can anchovy fillets in olive oil, drained
2 hard-boiled eggs, quartered
50g (2oz) black olives

To serve
30ml (2 tablespoons) freshly chopped parsley

granary French bread

1. Cook the French beans in the minimum of boiling water for about 5 minutes, until tender crisp. Drain and turn into a large bowl. Add tomatoes, spring onions and lettuce leaves with the celery and green pepper. Pour over the dressing. Toss to coat.

2. Arrange the dressed salad on an oval plate.
3. Top with the flaked tuna and anchovy fillets. Add the hard-boiled eggs and black olives, spacing them attractively.
4. Serve the salad immediately, sprinkled with the chopped parsley and accompanied with the granary French bread.

Super Pea & Cucumber Salad
Serves 4

A deliciously different salad. Frozen peas often taste better than fresh as they're picked and packed at their best to retain that just-picked freshness. Try this salad on a hot summer's day with cold chicken or barbecue dishes.

Preparation time: 10 mins
Cooking time: 5 mins

350g (12oz) frozen petits pois
3 spring onions, chopped
1/2 cucumber, peeled and diced
45ml (3 tablespoons) olive oil

30ml (2 tablespoons) white wine vinegar
5ml (1 teaspoon) concentrated mint sauce
2.5ml (1/2 teaspoon) caster sugar
Salt and freshly ground black pepper

1. Cook the peas until just cooked, according to directions on the packet, in the minimum of boiling water.
2. Drain peas and turn into a mixing bowl. Allow to cool.
3. Add the chopped spring onions and the diced cucumber to the bowl.
4. In a mug, combine the olive oil with the vinegar, mint sauce and caster sugar. Add a seasoning of salt and pepper. Whisk well with a fork and pour over peas.
5. Toss lightly to coat then serve immediately.

Waldorf Salad

Serves 4

A pretty salad made with apples, pears and walnuts. Serve as a starter with a lettuce garnish or as a salad.

Preparation time: 12 mins
Cooking time: 0

2 red-skinned English apples
2 green-skinned English
  apples
1 ripe Conference pear
Juice of 1 lemon
4 sticks celery, chopped
45ml (3 tablespoons) soured
  cream

45ml (3 tablespoons)
  reduced calorie
  mayonnaise
4 spring onions, chopped
Salt and freshly ground
  black pepper
50g (2oz) walnut pieces

To serve
lettuce leaves

1. Core and chop the red and green apples and peel, core and slice the pear. Put into a mixing bowl. Pour lemon juice over and toss to coat, then add celery.
2. Combine soured cream and mayonnaise. Stir in spring onions, a seasoning of salt and pepper and the walnuts.
3. Pour over fruit. Toss to coat.
4. Line a large plate with the lettuce leaves. Top with waldorf salad and serve immediately.

Special Family Salad
Serves 4

This delicious salad combines sweet sugar snap peas with chicory and Little Gem lettuce to make an interestingly different family salad that's so simple to prepare, yet pretty to serve.

Preparation time: 10 mins
Cooking time: 0

2 Little Gem lettuces
1 head chicory
175g (6oz) sugar snap peas

100g (4oz) cherry tomatoes, halved

For the dressing
1 clove garlic, crushed
5ml (1 teaspoon) caster sugar
5ml (1 teaspoon) Dijon mustard
Grated rind and juice of 1 lime

15ml (1 tablespoon) red wine vinegar
45ml (3 tablespoons) olive oil
15ml (1 tablespoon) freshly chopped coriander leaves
Salt and freshly ground black pepper

1. Separate the lettuce and chicory leaves and put them into a salad bowl. Add the sugar snap peas with the tomatoes.
2. Prepare the dressing. Put all ingredients for the dressing into a small bowl. Whisk well to form an emulsion. Alternatively, process all ingredients in a food processor for a few seconds.
3. When ready to serve, pour the dressing over the salad. Toss to coat and serve immediately.

Warm Potato Salad with Lemon & Sardines

Serves 4

New potatoes cooked in the microwave, then tossed whilst warm in a lemony vinaigrette taste simply wonderful. Serve with salad to make a complete quick lunch or supper.

Preparation time: 10 mins
Cooking time: 10 mins

450g (1lb) small new
   potatoes
2 sprigs fresh mint
3 stalks celery heart,
   chopped
1/2 small green pepper,
   seeded and chopped

120g (4¹/₄oz) can sardines in
   brine, drained and halved
15ml (1 tablespoon) snipped
   chives
15ml (1 tablespoon) freshly
   chopped parsley

For the vinaigrette
1 clove garlic, crushed
Rind and juice of 1/2 lemon
45ml (3 tablespoons) olive
  oil

Salt and freshly ground
  black pepper

1. Scrub the potatoes clean then prick each one once with a sharp knife.
2. Put the potatoes into a suitable microwave container. Add the mint and pour in 45ml (3 tablespoons) cold water. Cover with a lid or microwave cling film.
3. Microwave on 100%/FULL power for 7–9 minutes.
4. Stir the potatoes, re-cover and set aside for 5 minutes.
5. Meanwhile make the vinaigrette. Put the crushed garlic into a small bowl. Add the rind and juice from the lemon and the olive oil. Season with salt and pepper. Whisk well with a fork.
6. Drain potatoes and turn into a warmed serving dish. Add celery and green pepper. Immediately pour over vinaigrette. Toss to coat potatoes on all sides. Add the sardines.
7. Sprinkle with chives and parsley and serve immediately.

Bean & Sweetcorn Salad
with Chilli Dressing
Serves 4

Chillies are fast becoming very popular in everyday British food. When buying chillies, as a general rule, the thinner the´ chilli, the hotter. If you're new to chillies, remember to wear rubber gloves to seed and chop them and start by adding only one prepared chilli to your cooking, progressing to two or more as the family grow to appreciate the wonderful fiery flavour.

Preparation time: 10 mins
Cooking time: 5 mins

225g (8oz) frozen broad
   beans
225g (8oz) frozen sweetcorn
   kernels

1 red pepper, seeded and
   chopped
2 sun-dried tomatoes,
   drained and chopped

For the dressing
1 clove garlic, crushed
1.25ml (¹/₄ teaspoon)
   allspice
5ml (1 teaspoon) ground
   coriander
2 red chillies, chopped

60ml (4 tablespoons) orange
   juice
60ml (4 tablespoons) olive
   oil
Salt

To serve
30ml (2 tablespoons) freshly chopped parsley

1. Put the broad beans and sweetcorn kernels into a large pan. Pour over 300ml (10 fl oz) boiling water. Return to simmering point. Cover with a lid and simmer for

5 minutes, until beans are tender. Drain through a colander and turn into a mixing bowl. Set aside.

2. Prepare the dressing. Put all ingredients for the dressing into a screw-top jar and shake vigorously.

3. Add the red pepper and tomatoes to the salad, then pour over the dressing. Toss to coat, then serve the salad in an attractive dish, sprinkled with the chopped parsley.

Strawberry &
Courgette Salad
Serves 4

A refreshing salad that's stunning to look at. Serve for
summer buffets and special family lunches.

Preparation time: 15 mins + 15 mins for courgettes
Cooking time: 0

*4 medium size courgettes,
topped and tailed*
*350g (12oz) strawberries,
washed and hulled*
*Rind and juice of ½ large
orange*

*30ml (2 tablespoons) olive
oil*
*Salt and freshly ground
black pepper*
*5ml (1 teaspoon) granary
mustard*

To serve
30ml (2 tablespoons) freshly chopped parsley

1. Slice courgettes into ribbons, using a potato peeler and
   drawing it repeatedly down the long length of each
   courgette. Put courgette ribbons into a colander, sprinkle
   liberally with salt, then cover with a plate and weight such
   as a can of fruit. Set aside for 15 minutes to draw out the
   bitter juices. Rinse well under cold running water. Drain
   and turn into large mixing bowl.
2. Slice the strawberries and add to the bowl.
3. In a small bowl, combine the orange rind and juice with
   the olive oil, a seasoning of salt and pepper and the
   granary mustard. Whisk well with a fork, then pour
   dressing over salad. Toss to coat.
4. Serve immediately, sprinkled with the parsley.

Avocado & Tomato Salsa

Serves 4

A delicious side dish to serve on the buffet table. Useful, too, as an accompaniment to fish and meat dishes or try it with barbecue foods.

Preparation time: 10 mins
Cooking time: 0

1 large ripe avocado, stoned and peeled
Juice of ½ lemon
2 green chillies
2 shallots, peeled and chopped
397g (14oz) can chopped tomatoes

30ml (2 tablespoons) freshly chopped coriander
1 clove garlic, crushed
30ml (2 tablespoons) olive oil
Salt and freshly ground black pepper

1. Cut the avocado flesh into fairly small dice. Put into a mixing bowl.
2. Sprinkle over the lemon juice and toss to coat. (This will help prevent avocado from discolouring.)
3. Wearing rubber gloves to protect your hands, de-seed the chillies and discard the seeds.
4. Cut the chillies into fine shreds and add to the bowl.
5. Add all remaining ingredients. Stir well to combine.
6. Season to taste with a little salt and pepper, then set aside for 10 minutes or so to allow flavours to develop. Stir again just before serving.

Mackerel Pasta Salad
Serves 4

A good family meal when served with a green salad. Also excellent as a buffet party dish.

Preparation time: 15 mins
Cooking time: 10 mins

225g (8oz) multi-coloured
   pasta spirals
30ml (2 tablespoons) French
   dressing
45ml (3 tablespoons)
   reduced calorie
   mayonnaise
150ml (5 fl oz) Greek
   yoghurt
Grated rind of 1 lemon

225g (8oz) smoked mackerel
75g (3oz) peas, cooked and
   drained
2 eggs, size 2, hard-boiled
   and chopped
30ml (2 tablespoons) freshly
   chopped chives
Salt and freshly ground
   black pepper

To serve
30ml (2 tablespoons) freshly chopped parsley

1. Cook the pasta as directed. Drain thoroughly and turn into a mixing bowl. Whilst still hot, pour French dressing over and toss to coat. Set aside until cold.
2. In a separate large bowl, mix together the mayonnaise, yoghurt and lemon rind. Flake in the smoked mackerel, peas, hard-boiled eggs and chives. Season with a little salt and pepper.
3. Add the pasta. Toss to coat. Turn into serving dish and serve immediately, sprinkled with the freshly chopped parsley.

Tomato & Rice Salad

Serves 4

A colourful tasty way to use up any leftover rice. Boiled rice keeps well in the refrigerator for up to 5 days, so cook extra and use it in imaginative ways. Serve this rice salad with a green salad and smoked mackerel fillets for an almost instant tasty lunch.

Preparation time: 10 mins + 10 mins standing time
Cooking time: 0

450g (1lb) cooked, cold long grain rice, brown if possible (weighed cold)
1 large stick celery, diced
1 large courgette, diced
100g (4oz) dried apricots, chopped

400g (14oz) can peeled plum tomatoes
5ml (1 teaspoon) dried tarragon
30ml (2 tablespoons) single cream
Salt and freshly ground black pepper

To serve
50g (2oz) salted peanuts

1. Turn the rice into a large mixing bowl. Break down gently with a fork to separate grains.
2. Add celery, courgette and apricots to the rice.
3. Add tomatoes with their juice, chopping them roughly with a sharp knife and fork.
4. Add tarragon, single cream and a seasoning of salt and pepper. Toss ingredients together and turn into serving dish.
5. Set the salad aside for 10 minutes before serving, sprinkling the peanuts over on serving.

Rice Salad Ring
Serves 4

A delicious rice dish that can be served warm or cold. Serve the ring as a vegetable accompaniment, hot or cold, or fill with chicken or fish in a white sauce for a filling lunch or supper.

Preparation time: 5 mins
Cooking time: 10–12 mins

*250g (8oz) easy-cook
  American white rice
1 chicken stock cube
225g (8oz) frozen mixed
  vegetables (peas, carrots,
  beans, sweetcorn, red
  peppers)
15ml (1 tablespoon) freshly
  chopped parsley
300g (10oz) can chopped
  button mushrooms,
  drained*

*75g (3oz) lean ham,
  chopped
50g (2oz) white seedless
  grapes, halved
50g (2oz) sun-dried
  tomatoes, drained and
  chopped
30ml (2 tablespoons) olive
  oil
Salt and freshly ground
  black pepper*

1. Cook rice according to directions on the packet, adding the stock cube to the water. Drain and turn into a large mixing bowl.
2. Put the frozen vegetables into a small microwavable bowl. Add 30ml (2 tablespoons) cold water. Cover and micro-wave on 100%/FULL power for 5 minutes, stirring once halfway through.
3. Drain vegetables and add to rice with the parsley, mush-rooms, ham, grapes and tomatoes. Add oil and a season-ing of salt and pepper.
4. Toss well to coat then turn into a lightly oiled 20cm (8 inch) ring mould.

5. Press down well with the back of a spoon.
6. If serving cold, refrigerate until ready to serve. If serving hot, turn onto a serving plate and serve immediately.

Savoury Brown Rice

Serves 4

A well-flavoured rice dish that makes a filling accompaniment to chicken and fish or almost any recipe which has its own sauce such as fricassees, stews, etc.

Preparation time: 10 mins
Cooking time: 30 mins

225g (8oz) long grain brown rice
15ml (1 tablespoon) corn oil
100g (4oz) smoked bacon pieces, chopped
1 medium onion, chopped
1 medium courgette, sliced
100g (4oz) mushrooms, sliced
300ml (10 fl oz) chicken stock
50g (2oz) sultanas
10ml (2 teaspoons) dried parsley

1. Bring a large pan of water to the boil. Add the rice and return to simmer. Simmer, covered, for 20 minutes then drain the rice.
2. Meanwhile, heat the oil in a large frying pan.
3. Sauté the bacon and onion for 5 minutes, until onion softens. Add courgette and mushrooms and sauté for 3 minutes then stir in the drained rice, stock, sultanas and parsley. Stir well, bring to the boil, then cover and simmer for 10 minutes, until rice is tender.
4. Serve immediately.

Lemon Glazed Carrots
Serves 4

A well-flavoured way to present carrots that's a bit different; children will love this dish.

Preparation time: 10 mins
Cooking time: 10–12 mins

450g (1lb) carrots, peeled
  and sliced
Grated rind of 1/2 lemon
25g (1oz) butter
300ml (10 fl oz) vegetable
  stock

5ml (1 teaspoon) demerara
  sugar
Salt and freshly ground
  black pepper

To serve
15ml (1 tablespoon) freshly chopped parsley

1. Put carrots into a medium saucepan with the lemon rind.
2. Add butter and pour stock over. Sprinkle with sugar.
3. Bring to the boil, stirring now and again, then boil briskly, uncovered, stirring occasionally until stock is more or less absorbed and carrots are cooked and glazed (this will take 10–12 minutes).
4. Season to taste and serve immediately, sprinkled with the parsley.

Scalloped Potatoes

Serves 4

A tasty potato dish that cooks very speedily in the microwave. Make sure you choose an entrée dish that is grillproof.

Preparation time: 15 mins
Cooking time: 20 mins

40g (1¹/₂oz) butter
2 rashers streaky bacon, rinded and chopped
1 large onion, chopped
750g (1¹/₂lb) potatoes, peeled and very thinly sliced
5ml (1 teaspoon) dried oregano

Salt and freshly ground black pepper
90ml (6 tablespoons) milk
25g (1oz) Cheddar cheese, grated
2.5ml (¹/₂ teaspoon) paprika pepper

1. Melt the butter in a frying pan. Sauté the bacon and onion for 5 minutes, until softened and golden.
2. Grease a 1.2 litre (2 pint) entrée dish with a little butter. Layer the potatoes with the onion, bacon and oregano into the dish, ending with a layer of potatoes. Season each layer with salt and pepper.
3. Pour milk over potatoes, sprinkle evenly with cheese.
4. Cover with cling film and microwave on 100%/FULL power for 13 minutes.
5. Allow to stand for 5 minutes whilst you pre-heat the grill to medium hot. Check potato is tender in centre by piercing with a sharp knife. If not, cover again and return to microwave for 1–2 minutes.
6. Pop dish under the grill until cheese bubbles and browns. Sprinkle with paprika and serve immediately.

Baked Potatoes with Chicken & Corn

Serves 4

This is a firm favourite in our house. Starting the potatoes off in the microwave whilst you pre-heat the oven does ensure they're tender after 20 minutes in the oven and the skins are really crisp too if they're brushed with oil and sprinkled with salt before baking. Serve with salad.

Preparation time: 15 mins
Cooking time: 37–48 mins

4 × 175g (6oz) baking potatoes, scrubbed clean
15ml (1 tablespoon) rape seed oil
50g (2oz) sun-dried tomatoes, drained and chopped
Salt and freshly ground black pepper

100g (4oz) sliced chicken breast (from the deli), chopped
100g (4oz) frozen sweetcorn kernels, defrosted
45ml (3 tablespoons) milk
30ml (2 tablespoons) freshly chopped parsley

1. Pre-heat the oven to 230°C (450°F) gas mark 8.
2. Prick the potatoes with a fork, then brush all over with oil and sprinkle with salt.
3. Arrange the potatoes in a circle on a dinner plate. Microwave on 100%/FULL power for 13 minutes.
4. Transfer potatoes to roasting tin and bake in the pre-heated oven for 20–25 minutes, until tender and crisp.
5. Cut potatoes in half lengthways and scoop out pulp to within 5mm (¼ inch) of the skins. Turn into mixing bowl and mash with a fork.
6. Add tomatoes, a seasoning of salt and pepper, the chicken breast, sweetcorn, milk and parsley. Mix well to combine.

7. Pile back into skins and either return to oven for 10 minutes or microwave on 100%/FULL power for 4–5 minutes, until thoroughly hot.
8. Serve immediately.

Stir-fried Mushrooms & Courgettes

Serves 4

A slightly different vegetable dish that goes equally well with pasta dishes, chicken, beef and pork. Good, too, as a snack lunch with poached eggs and grated cheese.

Preparation time: 5 mins
Cooking time: 10 mins

30ml (2 tablespoons) sunflower oil
225g (8oz) chestnut or button mushrooms
350g (12oz) courgettes, sliced
15ml (1 tablespoon) lemon juice

45ml (3 tablespoons) freshly chopped parsley or 15ml (1 tablespoon) dried parsley
Salt and freshly ground black pepper

1. Heat the oil in a large frying pan.
2. Add mushrooms and courgettes and stir-fry over a fairly high heat for 8–10 minutes, until tender and just starting to brown.
3. Stir in the lemon juice, parsley and a seasoning of salt and pepper. Heat, stirring for one more minute.
4. Serve immediately.

Courgette &
Beansprout Stir-fry
Serves 4

Even if you're in a hurry, slice the courgettes, place in a colander and sprinkle liberally with salt. Set aside for 10–15 minutes to allow juices to run, then rinse well with cold running water to get rid of any bitterness. Serve with almost any meat, poultry or fish dish.

Preparation time: 10 mins + 10–15 mins for courgettes
Cooking time: 11 mins

450g (1lb) courgettes, sliced
30ml (2 tablespoons) olive oil
1 red-skinned onion, chopped

1 clove garlic, crushed
100g (4oz) beansprouts
Grated rind and juice of 1 orange

To serve
30ml (2 tablespoons) freshly chopped parsley

1. Prepare courgettes as directed in the introduction above. Drain and blot dry on absorbent kitchen paper.
2. Heat oil in a wok or large frying pan. Add onion and garlic and stir-fry for 2–3 minutes.
3. Add courgettes and stir-fry over a high heat for about 7 minutes, until starting to brown.
4. Add beansprouts with the orange rind and juice. Stir-fry for 1–2 minutes then serve sprinkled with the chopped parsley.

Main Courses

Chicken & Passata Stove Top Casserole
Serves 4

Succulent chicken breasts in a rich tomato sauce with colourful vegetables which still retain their bite. Serve this family casserole with boiled rice, creamy mashed potato or just with warm Italian ciabatta bread and a salad. Good enough for entertaining friends.

Preparation time: 10 mins
Cooking time: 40 mins

30ml (2 tablespoons) olive oil
4 boneless chicken breasts, about 200g (7oz) each
1 onion, peeled and chopped
1 clove garlic, crushed (optional)
1 green pepper, seeded and thinly sliced
225g (8oz) carrots, cut into matchsticks
100g (4oz) button mushrooms, sliced
550g (1¼lb) jar passata
Salt and freshly ground black pepper
1 bay leaf

1. Heat the oil in a large stove top casserole, then quickly brown the chicken breasts on all sides, until just golden. Using tongs, remove chicken to a dinner plate.
2. Add onion and garlic to the pan and sauté for 3 minutes until softened. Add the green pepper and the carrots. Sauté for a further 3 minutes. Stir in the mushrooms.
3. Top vegetables with the browned chicken pieces. Pour over the passata and season lightly with salt and pepper. Add the bay leaf.
4. Cover with a lid and simmer for 30–35 minutes, until chicken is tender. Remove bay leaf before serving.

Microwave Country Chicken Casserole
Serves 4

This warming chicken dish is good family fodder on a cold autumn or winter's night. Try the casserole with boiled rice, steaming pasta or jacket potatoes.

Preparation time: 10 mins
Cooking time: 25 mins

75g (3oz) streaky bacon
1 medium onion, peeled and chopped
225g (8oz) mushrooms, chopped

4 chicken quarters (about 700g (1½lb) total weight), skinned
400g (14oz) can chopped tomatoes
30ml (2 tablespoons) tomato purée
300ml (10 fl oz) chicken stock
5ml (1 teaspoon) dried oregano
Salt and freshly ground black pepper
20ml (4 teaspoons) cornflour

To serve
30ml (2 tablespoons) freshly chopped parsley

1. Chop the bacon, discarding the rind and put into a 2.25 litre (4 pint) microwavable casserole dish.
2. Add the onion, mushrooms, chicken, chopped tomatoes, tomato purée, stock and oregano. Season with a little salt and pepper.
3. Stir well, then cover with a lid and microwave on 100%/FULL power for 10 minutes. Stir to re-arrange chicken.
4. Re-cover and microwave on 100%/FULL power for 12 minutes or until chicken is tender. Set aside, covered, for 5 minutes then lift chicken portions onto serving dish. Keep warm.
5. Blend cornflour with a little water and stir into casserole. Microwave, uncovered, on 100%/FULL power for 3–4 minutes, stirring once during cooking, until slightly thickened.
6. Pour the hot sauce over the chicken portions and serve immediately, sprinkled with the chopped parsley.

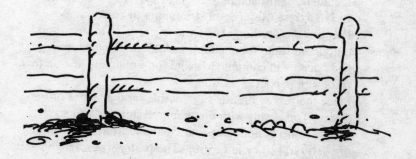

Turkey en Croûte
Serves 4–6

An extremely easy recipe for a special family occasion. Whilst
the turkey cooks you have time to prepare a couple of salads
and a quick dessert. A firm favourite in our house.

Preparation time: 15 mins
Cooking time: 45 mins

*500g (1lb 2oz) pack fresh
    puff pastry*

*4 × 100g (4oz) turkey
    breasts*

For the stuffing
*15ml (1 tablespoon) corn oil
1 medium onion, chopped
100g (4oz) mushrooms,
    chopped
15ml (1 tablespoon) dried
    parsley*

*100g (4oz) back bacon,
    rinded and chopped
Freshly ground black pepper
1 egg, size 3, beaten*

1. Pre-heat the oven to 220°C (425°F) gas mark 7.
2. On a lightly floured board, roll the pastry out to a
   rectangle, approximately 30 × 40cm (12 × 16 inches).
   Leave to rest. Reserve any trimmings of pastry.
3. Prepare the stuffing. Heat the oil in a frying pan, add
   onion and sauté for 2 minutes. Add mushrooms, parsley
   and bacon and continue to sauté for 4 minutes. Season to
   taste with pepper. Set aside.
4. Place the turkey breasts side by side on the centre of the
   pastry. Top evenly with the prepared stuffing.
5. With a sharp knife, make four cuts, one from each corner
   of pastry to turkey in centre. (The pastry will resemble 4
   envelope flaps.) Brush edges with beaten egg.
6. Bring up ends and fold around turkey. Bring up sides to
   meet. Seal edges.

7. Cut leaves from pastry trimmings and use to decorate croûte. Place on baking sheet, keeping join on underside of croûte. Brush with egg.
8. Bake for approximately 40 minutes, until golden.
9. Delicious hot or cold, served cut in slices.

Easy Stir-fry
Serves 4

This stir-fry is quick and easy to prepare and cook. Good enough for an impromptu dinner party and excellent just for a family supper, serve with boiled rice or noodles.

Preparation time: 10 mins
Cooking time: 6 mins

30ml (2 tablespoons) rape seed oil

225g (8oz) turkey breast fillet, thinly sliced

225g (8oz) lean gammon, thinly sliced

1 red pepper, seeded and chopped

75g (3oz) button mushrooms, sliced

4 spring onions, cut into shreds

100g (4oz) fresh or frozen mangetout, trimmed

150g (5oz) jar sweet and sour sauce

To serve
15ml (1 tablespoon) freshly chopped parsley

1. Heat oil in a wok or large frying pan.
2. Stir-fry turkey and gammon for approximately 3 minutes.
3. Add red pepper, mushrooms, onions and mangetout. Stir-fry for a further 2–3 minutes.
4. Stir in sauce and heat through thoroughly, stirring. Serve immediately sprinkled with the parsley.

Neapolitan Lamb

Serves 4

Stir-frying is a quick and popular way to cook a tasty main course. Ensure that you have everything ready prepared before you start to cook. Stir-fry sauce is readily available in glass jars in the supermarkets, usually near the rice and pasta sections.

Preparation time: 15 mins
Cooking time: 7 mins

15ml (1 tablespoon)
  sunflower oil
1 clove garlic, crushed
1 medium onion, chopped
2 courgettes, sliced

3 boneless lamb steaks,
  trimmed and cut into strips
100g (4oz) mushrooms,
  sliced
150g (5oz) jar stir-fry sauce
  of choice

To serve
boiled spaghetti or rice

1. Heat oil in a wok or large frying pan. Add garlic and onion and stir-fry for 2 minutes, stirring. Add courgettes and lamb and stir-fry over a fairly high heat for 2–3 minutes, until meat is browned on all sides.
2. Add mushrooms and continue to stir-fry for 2 minutes.
3. Stir in the sauce and gently heat through.
4. Serve immediately on a bed of steaming spaghetti or rice.

Chinese Lamb
Stir-fry
Serves 4

Families love stir-fries and this recipe uses tender and succulent leg of lamb steaks to create a tasty dish with an Oriental flavour. Serve with boiled rice and a green salad.

Preparation time: 10 mins + marinating time
Cooking time: 8 mins

*450g (1lb) boneless leg of
   lamb steaks, cut into strips*

For the marinade
1 clove garlic, crushed
*2.5cm (1 inch) piece root
   ginger, grated*
*5ml (1 teaspoon) Chinese
   five spice powder*

*15ml (1 tablespoon) soy
   sauce*
Juice of 1 lime
5ml (1 teaspoon) clear honey

Additions
10ml (2 teaspoons) olive oil
1 courgette, sliced
100g (4oz) beansprouts

*100g (4oz) white cabbage,
   shredded*
100g (4oz) frozen peas
5ml (1 teaspoon) cornflour

1. Put lamb into a large mixing bowl. In a small jug, combine all ingredients for the marinade, stir well and pour over lamb. Toss to coat, then set aside for 10 minutes.
2. Heat oil in a wok or large frying pan. Add meat, reserving any juices. Stir-fry over a fairly high heat for 3–4 minutes.
3. Add courgette, beansprouts, cabbage and peas. Stir-fry for a further 3 minutes.
4. Blend cornflour with remaining marinade. Pour into wok

and continue to cook, stirring, until sauce boils and thickens.
5. Serve immediately.

Baked Pork
with Rice

Serves 4

A very easy dish to prepare, giving you time to throw a salad together and make a quick pud whilst the pork cooks to perfection in the oven. Serve with French bread and a colourful salad.

Preparation time: 10 mins
Cooking time: 45–50 mins

1 onion, finely chopped
1 stick celery, chopped
397g (14oz) can chopped tomatoes
15ml (1 tablespoon) tomato purée
1.25–2.5ml (¼–½ teaspoon) crushed dried chillies (according to how hot you like things)
10ml (2 teaspoons) dried parsley
50g (2oz) long grain white rice

150ml (5 fl oz) stock
Salt and freshly ground black pepper
10ml (2 teaspoons) sunflower oil
4 pork leg fillet steaks
1 red pepper, seeded and chopped
1 green pepper, seeded and chopped
50g (2oz) dried apricots, chopped

1. Pre-heat the oven to 180°C (350°F) gas mark 4.
2. Put onion, celery, tomatoes, tomato purée, chillies, parsley, rice and stock into a 2.25 litre (4 pint) stove top and ovenproof casserole. Season with salt and pepper. Bring to the boil, then remove from heat.
3. Meanwhile, heat the oil in a frying pan and quickly seal pork on both sides, until browned.

4. Add pork to casserole, in a single layer. Cover casserole with a lid.
5. Bake for 20 minutes. Stir in peppers and apricots. Re-cover and return to oven for a further 20–25 minutes, until pork is cooked and rice is tender.
6. Serve immediately.

Spicy Minced Pork

Serves 4

A delicious mixture of pork with vegetables and spices. Good enough for a family birthday lunch or supper, serve with pasta, rice or potatoes and a tossed mixed salad.

Preparation time: 15 mins
Cooking time: 30 mins

15ml (1 tablespoon) sunflower oil
2 leeks, cleaned and sliced
225g (8oz) carrots, diced
225g (8oz) lean minced pork
15ml (1 tablespoon) cornflour
600ml (1 pint) chicken stock
2 small eating apples, peeled, cored and chopped
5ml (1 teaspoon) dried mixed herbs
15ml (1 tablespoon) curry paste
15ml (1 tablespoon) soy sauce
15ml (1 tablespoon) tomato purée
100g (4oz) mushrooms, chopped

1. Heat the oil in a large stove top casserole dish, then sauté the leeks and carrots for 5 minutes, until softened slightly. Add the mince and continue to sauté for a further 5–7 minutes over a fairly high heat, until browned.
2. Blend cornflour to a smooth paste with 30ml (2 tablespoons) of the stock and stir into the casserole with remaining stock and rest of ingredients.
3. Bring to the boil, stirring then cover and simmer gently for 20 minutes, until carrots are tender.
4. Serve with pasta, rice or potatoes.

Crispy Topped
Pork Chops

Serves 4

The tomato and Parmesan-flavoured topping is delicious with succulent pork chops. Serve with salad and new potatoes cooked in their skins.

Preparation time: 10 mins
Cooking time: 25–30 mins

4 boneless pork chops

For the topping
75g (3oz) fresh brown breadcrumbs

2 tomatoes, peeled and chopped, discarding seeds

50g (2oz) mushrooms, finely chopped

5ml (1 teaspoon) dried basil
Salt and freshly ground black pepper
1 egg, size 4, beaten
15ml (1 tablespoon) grated Parmesan cheese

1. Pre-heat the grill to medium hot. Lightly oil the grill rack.
2. Grill the chops for approximately 20–25 minutes, turning frequently, until juices run clear and pork is cooked through.
3. Meanwhile, prepare the topping. In a mixing bowl combine breadcrumbs, chopped tomato, mushrooms and basil. Season with a little salt and pepper and mix well. Add egg and mix to bind together.
4. Spoon topping evenly onto chops and press it on with the back of a fork. You will have a fairly generous amount for each chop. Sprinkle the chops with the Parmesan cheese then continue to grill for 5 minutes, until golden.
5. Serve immediately.

Speedy Pork with Spinach, Chick Peas & Corn
Serves 4

A lovely garlicky dish with a robust flavour. Serve with chunks of warmed wholemeal bread or a dish of creamy mashed potatoes if you have a little more time.

Preparation time: 15 mins
Cooking time: 17 mins

30ml (2 tablespoons) olive oil

1 medium onion, peeled and chopped

450g (1lb) pork leg fillet, cubed

4 plump cloves garlic, crushed

2.5ml (1/2 teaspoon) dried crushed chillies

Salt and freshly ground black pepper

225g (8oz) frozen chopped leaf spinach

415g (14 1/2oz) can chick peas, drained

100g (4oz) frozen sweetcorn kernels

150ml (5 fl oz) chicken stock

1. Heat the oil in a large, fairly deep frying pan.
2. Add onion, pork, garlic and chillies. Sauté over a medium heat for about 7 minutes, being careful not to allow garlic to burn.
3. Season with a little salt and pepper. Stir in spinach, chick peas and sweetcorn. Pour over the stock.
4. Bring to the boil, then cover and simmer for 10 minutes. Serve immediately.

Sausage & Bean Bake

Serves 4–6

A rich, filling dish that's deliciously crunchy and all cooked in one pot, so there's not too much washing up afterwards. Serve with a mixed leaf salad.

Preparation time: 15 mins
Cooking time: 35 mins

30ml (2 tablespoons) sunflower oil
450g (1lb) pork sausages with herbs
1 large onion, peeled and chopped
1 clove garlic, crushed
6 stalks celery (about 450g (1lb)), washed and finely chopped
1 red pepper, seeded and chopped
200ml (7 fl oz) beef stock
400g (14oz) can plum tomatoes in juice

30ml (2 tablespoons) tomato purée
10ml (2 teaspoons) paprika
15ml (1 tablespoon) soy sauce
400g (14oz) can red kidney beans, drained
75g (3oz) frozen sweetcorn kernels
8 slices French bread (1 baguette, thickly sliced)
50g (2oz) Gouda cheese, grated

1. Heat the oil in a large flameproof casserole, then fry the sausages on all sides until browned. Lift onto a dinner plate and set aside.
2. Add onion, garlic and celery to the casserole and sauté for 5–7 minutes, until the vegetables soften. Cut each sausage in half and return to casserole.

3. Add the red pepper, stock, tomatoes with any juice, tomato purée, paprika, soy sauce and the red kidney beans. Stir well, then cover and simmer for 20–25 minutes, until vegetables are just tender but celery still retains a bite. Stir in the sweetcorn and simmer, covered, for 5 minutes. Pre-heat the grill to medium heat.

4. Arrange slices of French bread around the top of the casserole, to form a circle around the edge, overlapping if necessary. Sprinkle with grated cheese and grill for 2–3 minutes until cheese melts. Serve immediately.

Sausage & Bramley Plait

Serves 4–6

The Bramley apples give a wonderful tangy flavour to this very special family pie. It's rather like eating sausages with chutney. Serve on a cold winter's evening for a warming treat or take it on picnics to impress friends! Serve with salad.

Preparation time: 20 mins
Cooking time: 35 mins

15ml (1 tablespoon) rape seed oil
1 medium onion, peeled and chopped
450g (1lb) Bramley apples, peeled, cored and diced
225g (8oz) courgettes, sliced
100g (4oz) mushrooms, chopped
5ml (1 teaspoon) dried thyme
25g (1oz) sultanas
Salt and freshly ground black pepper
500g (1lb 2oz) pack fresh puff pastry
450g (1lb) pork sausagemeat

To glaze
1 egg, size 3, beaten

1. Pre-heat the oven to 200°C (400°F) gas mark 6.
2. Heat the oil in a large frying pan, then sauté the onion, apples, courgettes and mushrooms for about 10 minutes, until apples soften. Add the thyme, sultanas and a seasoning of salt and pepper. Stir well and set aside to cool.
3. On a lightly floured board, roll the pastry out to a rectangle approximately 30 × 35cm (12 × 14 inches).
4. Lay the pastry on a baking sheet and, using the back of a knife, mark into three equal panels lengthways.
5. Roll the sausagemeat out on the floured board to fit the

centre panel, but leave 1.25cm (½ inch) border of pastry all round. Lift sausagemeat onto centre panel.

6. Spoon apple and vegetable mixture evenly over sausage-meat.

7. Cut 1.25cm (½ inch) strips, on the slant, down each of the pastry side panels, then cross the strips over the sausage and vegetables to form a plait. Brush with egg.

8. Bake for 35 minutes, until golden.

9. Serve hot or cold.

Curried Beef Cobbler
Serves 4

Curried mince with a scone topping makes a complete meal that everyone enjoys. Serve with a mixed salad or stir-fried vegetables.

Note: If you do not have time to make the scones, serve the curried mince at the end of step 3 with boiled rice or warmed French bread.

Preparation time: 15 mins
Cooking time: 45 mins or 20 mins without scone topping

2 rashers streaky bacon, rinded and chopped
450g (1lb) lean minced beef
1 medium onion, peeled and chopped
15ml (1 tablespoon) medium curry powder

10ml (2 teaspoons) plain flour
1 clove garlic, crushed
30ml (2 tablespoons) tomato purée
2 courgettes, sliced
300ml (10 fl oz) beef stock

For the topping
175g (6oz) self-raising flour
5ml (1 teaspoon) baking powder
Pinch salt
50g (2oz) polyunsaturated margarine
1 egg, size 3

30ml (2 tablespoons) milk
30ml (2 tablespoons) freshly chopped parsley
A little milk for brushing
25g (1oz) Cheddar cheese, grated

1. Pre-heat the oven to 220°C (425°F) gas mark 7.
2. Heat a large non-stick frying pan, then dry fry the bacon with the minced beef for about 5 minutes, stirring frequently until beef browns. Add the onion and sauté for a further 5 minutes.
3. Stir in the curry powder and flour. Cook, stirring, for

1 minute then add the garlic, tomato purée, courgettes and stock. Bring to the boil, stirring, then cover and simmer for 15 minutes.

4. Make the scone topping. Put flour, baking powder and salt into food processor. Cube margarine and add to machine. Process until mixture resembles fine breadcrumbs. Beat the egg and milk together and add with the parsley. Process to form a soft dough.

5. Turn dough onto floured board and roll out to about 1.25cm (½ inch) thick. Cut into 4cm (1½ inch) circles using a pastry cutter or egg cup.

6. Turn mince mixture into a shallow oval dish then arrange scones around edge of mince, overlapping if necessary. Brush scones with milk and sprinkle with cheese.

7. Bake for 20 minutes or until topping is well risen and golden brown. Serve immediately.

Pizza Bolognese
Serves 4

A quickly made French bread pizza with the extra flavour of real minced beef. Serve straight from the oven with a tossed mixed salad. Teenagers love this meaty meal.

Preparation time: 10 mins
Cooking time: 27–29 mins

1 large French stick

For the beef topping
350g (12oz) lean minced beef
2 rashers streaky bacon,
  rinded and chopped
440g (16oz) jar Ragu pasta
  sauce, traditional style
75g (3oz) button
  mushrooms, sliced

2 medium size tomatoes,
  sliced thinly
15ml (1 tablespoon) dried
  basil or oregano
75g (3oz) Cheddar cheese,
  grated

1. Pre-heat the oven to 230°C (450°F) gas mark 8.
2. Prepare the topping. In a large non-stick frying pan, dry fry the beef with the bacon for 5 minutes over a high heat, stirring frequently until the beef starts to brown.
3. Stir in the Ragu sauce and the mushrooms. Bring to simmering point, stirring, then cover and simmer for 12 minutes.
4. Cut the French stick in half, then cut each half into two pieces across centre. Arrange two halves of French bread on each of two baking sheets, using crumpled foil to hold bread in position, if necessary.
5. Divide meat sauce between bread bases, spreading it over evenly.
6. Top with tomato slices and sprinkle with the basil or oregano.

7. Sprinkle with the grated cheese.
8. Bake for 10–12 minutes until cheese melts and turns golden.
9. Serve immediately, cut into slices, accompanied by a mixed salad.

Tomato &
Kidney Turbigo
Serves 4

A filling lunch or supper dish which is ideal for a cold winter's evening. Kidneys are highly nutritious, but don't overcook them as they tend to toughen. Serve with boiled rice and a green salad.

Preparation time: 10 mins
Cooking time: 22 mins

30ml (2 tablespoons) oil
1 medium size onion, chopped
225g (8oz) lambs' kidneys, skinned, cored and halved
100g (4oz) button mushrooms, halved
30ml (2 tablespoons) medium sherry

300ml (10 fl oz) passata
5ml (1 teaspoon) dried dill
60ml (4 tablespoons) soured cream
Salt and freshly ground black pepper
3 slices brown bread
30ml (2 tablespoons) freshly chopped parsley

1. Heat the oil in a large shallow frying pan, add the onion and sauté for 5 minutes until softened.
2. Add the kidneys and mushrooms and fry over a medium heat for 5–6 minutes, stirring frequently.
3. Stir in the sherry, passata, dill and soured cream. Season with a little salt and pepper.
4. Bring slowly to the boil, then cover and simmer for 10 minutes, stirring occasionally.
5. Meanwhile toast the bread on both sides until lightly golden.

6. To serve, turn the kidney mixture into a warm serving dish. Cut the toast into triangles and arrange round edge of dish.

7. Sprinkle with parsley and serve immediately.

Pan Fried Cod

Serves 4

Cod steaks cooked with lemon juice and a few snipped herbs are a long way removed from battered or breadcrumb-coated fish. Try this recipe for sheer taste – the family will love you for it! Serve with oven chips and a crisp green salad.

Preparation time: 5 mins
Cooking time: 10 mins

Grated rind of 1 lemon
40g (1¹/₂oz) plain wholemeal flour
10ml (2 teaspoons) dried parsley
Salt and freshly ground black pepper

700g (1¹/₂lb) skinned and filleted fresh cod (4 largish cod fillets)
60ml (4 tablespoons) sunflower oil

To serve
wedges of lemon

1. Mix the lemon rind with the flour and dried parsley on a dinner plate. Season with the salt and pepper.
2. Dip the cod fillets into the flour so that they become coated on all sides. Shake off excess and transfer to a clean dinner plate.
3. Heat the oil in a shallow frying pan then fry the fillets, two at a time, for about 2 minutes each side, until golden and no longer opaque-looking.
4. Drain on absorbent kitchen paper before serving. (Place the first two fillets in a warm oven whilst you fry remaining two.)
5. Serve the cod garnished with the lemon wedges.

Ratatouille
with Haddock
Serves 4

A complete meal cooked in one dish that's fairly low on calories too. Serve with warm French bread or rolls for a filling lunch or supper.

Preparation time: 10 mins + 10–15 mins for courgettes
Cooking time: 35 mins

3 courgettes, diced
1 small aubergine, diced
Salt and freshly ground
* black pepper*
30ml (2 tablespoons) rape
* seed oil*
2 red-skinned onions, peeled
* and chopped*
2 cloves garlic, crushed
1 medium size yellow
* pepper, seeded and*
* chopped*

15ml (1 tablespoon) dried
* mixed herbs*
550g (1¼lb) jar passata
30ml (2 tablespoons)
* vegetable purée*
4 × 175g (6oz) haddock fillets
50g (2oz) Cheddar cheese,
* grated*
15ml (1 tablespoon) freshly
* chopped parsley*

1. Layer courgettes and aubergine into a colander. Sprinkle liberally with salt and set aside for 10–15 minutes, then rinse well with cold water and drain.
2. Heat the oil in a large, stove top casserole. Add onions and garlic and sauté for 5 minutes until onion softens.
3. Add courgettes, aubergine and pepper to the pan and sauté for a further 3 minutes.
4. Sprinkle over the mixed herbs, then pour over the passata. Add the vegetable purée and a seasoning of salt and pepper.

5. Bring to the boil, stirring then simmer, covered, for 20 minutes. Stir well, top with the fish, in a single layer. Cover and continue to simmer for 5–7 minutes until the fish flakes and is no longer opaque.
6. Sprinkle with cheese and parsley and serve immediately (the cheese will melt almost instantly).

Quick Salmon & Tuna Pie

Serves 4

A filling and quite luxurious fishy pie that's a firm favourite in our house. Serve with salad or peas and mashed potatoes if time allows.

Preparation time: 15 mins
Cooking time: 30–35 mins

25g (1oz) polyunsaturated
  margarine
25g (1oz) plain flour
300ml (10 fl oz)
  semi-skimmed milk
Salt and freshly ground
  black pepper
75g (3oz) frozen sweetcorn
  kernels

212g (7¹/₂oz) can pink or red
  salmon, drained
185g (6¹/₂oz) can tuna
  chunks in oil, drained
1 medium size ripe tomato,
  thinly sliced
275g (10oz) packet frozen
  puff pastry, defrosted
Milk for brushing

1. Pre-heat the oven to 200°C (400°F) gas mark 6.
2. Melt the margarine in a medium saucepan. Stir in flour and cook for about 1 minute, stirring. Remove from heat and gradually stir in the milk. Season with a little salt and pepper.
3. Return pan to heat and bring to boil, stirring continuously until a creamy sauce results. Add sweetcorn to sauce and stir.
4. Remove skin and bones from salmon and flake flesh into the sauce with the tuna. Mix gently and pour into a 17.5cm (7 inch) pie dish.
5. Top pie filling evenly with tomato slices.
6. Roll out pastry a little larger than the dish. Cut off a strip of pastry about 1.25cm (½ inch) wide.
7. Dampen edge of pie dish then top edge with strip of

pastry. Dampen pastry edge then lift pastry lid onto pie.
8. Slash one hole in centre to allow steam to escape.
9. Use any trimmings to make leaves and arrange on pie.
10. Stand pie on baking sheet. Brush all over with milk.
11. Bake for 30–35 minutes, until well risen and golden brown. Serve immediately.

Baked Potatoes with Coleslaw & Tuna

Serves 4

A meal in themselves, baked potatoes are ideal for so many occasions. Encourage everyone to eat the skins which are an excellent source of fibre – they taste delicious, too.

Preparation time: 10 mins
Cooking time: 38 mins

4 × 275g (10oz) baking potatoes, scrubbed clean

For the filling
175g (6oz) white cabbage, finely shredded
1 carrot, grated
1 stick celery, finely chopped
45ml (3 tablespoons) reduced calorie mayonnaise
50g (2oz) dried apricots or dates, chopped

Grated rind and juice of 1/2 small orange
Salt and freshly ground black pepper
198g (7oz) can tuna in brine, drained
50g (2oz) Double Gloucester cheese, grated

1. Prick the potatoes with a fork, then arrange in a circle, on a dinner plate. Microwave on 100%/FULL power for 13 minutes.
2. Meanwhile, pre-heat the oven to 230°C (450°F) gas mark 8.
3. Transfer potatoes to a greased roasting tin and bake in the pre-heated oven for 20–25 minutes until tender.
4. Meanwhile, prepare the filling. Put cabbage, carrot and celery into a mixing bowl. Add mayonnaise, dried apricots or dates, orange rind and juice and a seasoning of salt and

pepper. Mix well and set aside.
5. When potatoes are cooked, split them open and top with the coleslaw and drained, flaked tuna.
6. Sprinkle each filled potato with a little grated cheese and serve immediately.

Pasta Perfect

Serves 4

A super Italian dish that uses pasta and potatoes cooked with cream for a tasty lunch or supper. Suitable for vegetarians, serve this fast dish with halved or sliced tomatoes tossed in a vinaigrette and topped with torn basil leaves.

Preparation time: 6 mins
Cooking time: 35–40 mins

225g (8oz) dried pasta shapes
225g (8oz) carrots, sliced
450g (1lb) white potatoes, scrubbed clean and diced
2 medium Cox's apples, peeled, cored and diced
1 clove garlic, crushed
Salt and freshly ground black pepper

15ml (1 tablespoon) dried basil
15ml (1 tablespoon) olive oil
150g (5oz) medium Cheddar cheese, grated
425ml (15 fl oz) single cream
50g (2oz) mature Cheddar cheese, grated
25g (1oz) fresh breadcrumbs

1. Cook the pasta in plenty of boiling water, until *al dente* according to directions on the packet. Stir pasta once or twice during cooking to prevent it sticking.
2. Put carrots and potatoes into a 1.75 litre (3 pint) mixing bowl. Add 45ml (3 tablespoons) water. Cover with microwave cling film and microwave on 100%/FULL power for 9 minutes. Stir, then allow to stand, covered, for 2 minutes. Drain vegetables and return to bowl.
3. Drain pasta and add to carrots and potatoes. Add the apples, garlic, a seasoning of salt and pepper, basil, olive oil and the medium cheese. Gently heat the cream in a medium saucepan, until thoroughly hot. Pour cream over pasta mixture. Stir to mix.

4. Transfer mixture to a 2.25 litre (4 pint) shallow, oven-proof dish.
5. Sprinkle with the mature cheese and breadcrumbs.
6. Brown under a pre-heated grill. Serve immediately.

Vegetable Goulash

Serves 4–6

Served with rice, or just chunks of wholemeal bread, this delicious veggie meal will be popular with just about everyone.

Preparation time: 15 mins
Cooking time: 25–30 mins

30ml (2 tablespoons) rape seed oil
1 medium onion, chopped
1 large stick celery, finely chopped
2 courgettes, sliced
2 medium carrots, sliced
225g (8oz) potatoes, scrubbed clean and diced
225g (8oz) parsnips, peeled and sliced
225g (8oz) cauliflower florets
397g (14oz) can plum tomatoes
100g (4oz) button mushrooms, sliced
30ml (2 tablespoons) tomato purée
10ml (2 teaspoons) paprika
300ml (10 fl oz) vegetable stock
A few drops chilli sauce
Salt
400g (14oz) can red kidney beans, drained
15ml (1 tablespoon) cornflour
45ml (3 tablespoons) soured cream

To serve
30ml (2 tablespoons) freshly chopped parsley

1. Heat the oil in a large casserole or saucepan.
2. Add onion and celery and sauté for 5 minutes until softened.
3. Add courgettes, carrots, potatoes, parsnips and cauliflower. Sauté for 2–3 minutes then add tomatoes with their juice, mushrooms, tomato purée, paprika, stock and chilli sauce. Season with a little salt, stir well and bring to the boil.

4. Cover and simmer for 20–25 minutes, stirring occasionally, until vegetables are tender. Stir in kidney beans.
5. Mix cornflour to a smooth paste with a little water and stir in. Simmer for 2–3 minutes, stirring until slightly thickened. Remove from heat. Stir in cream and serve sprinkled with the chopped parsley.

Tomato, Ham & Cheese Pancakes

Serves 4

Pancakes are frequently served in France for main course meals, stuffed with tasty fillings. Try this ham and cheese version for a quick lunch.

Preparation time: 15 mins
Cooking time: approx. 20 mins

50g (2oz) plain flour
50g (2oz) wholemeal flour
Salt and freshly ground
   black pepper

1 egg, size 3
300ml (10 fl oz) skimmed
   milk
Oil for frying

For the filling
3 medium size ripe tomatoes,
   peeled and chopped
50g (2oz) lean ham, diced

50g (2oz) half-fat Cheddar
   cheese, grated
100g (4oz) frozen sweetcorn
   kernels, defrosted

To finish
50g (2oz) half-fat Cheddar cheese, grated

To serve
salad garnish

1. Pre-heat the oven to 200°C (400°F) gas mark 6.
2. Sift the plain and wholemeal flour into a mixing bowl, adding any bran that is left in the sieve.
3. Add a seasoning of salt and pepper, then make a well in the centre of the flour. Add the egg and skimmed milk.
4. Using a wooden spoon, gradually beat the flour into the liquid to make a smooth batter.
5. Lightly oil a 18cm (7 inch) frying pan. Pour in 45ml (3 tablespoons) of the batter and cook for 2 minutes until golden. Toss or flip pancake over with a palette knife and cook second side for a further 1–2 minutes until golden. Make 8 pancakes, oiling the pan each time.
6. Fold pancakes in half and half again to form pouches.
7. In a mixing bowl, combine all ingredients for the filling. Divide between the pancakes evenly.
8. Arrange in a single layer in a large ovenproof dish. Sprinkle with remaining cheese then bake for 10 minutes.
9. Serve immediately, with a salad garnish.

Desserts

Blackcurrant & Redcurrant Fool

Serves 4

A light fruity dessert that's delicious in the autumn and winter months.

Preparation time: 15 mins
Cooking time: 5–7 mins

225g (8oz) redcurrants, removed from stem (frozen will do)
225g (8oz) blackcurrants, removed from stem (frozen will do)

50g (2oz) light muscovado brown sugar
425g (15oz) can ready made custard
45ml (3 tablespoons) Greek yoghurt

To serve
4 sprigs of redcurrants

1. Put the redcurrants and blackcurrants into a large saucepan. Add 30ml (2 tablespoons) water. Sprinkle over the sugar. Cover with a lid.
2. Simmer for 5–7 minutes, until fruit is soft, stirring occasionally. Allow to cool for 10 minutes, then pass through a sieve into a mixing bowl.
3. Using a metal spoon, fold the custard and the Greek yoghurt into the fruit purée.
4. Divide the fool between four wine glasses or sundae dishes and chill in the fridge until ready to serve.
5. Serve each dessert topped with a sprig of redcurrants.

Melba Fool

Serves 4

Soft fruits with fromage frais and honey make a wonderful creamy dessert that's healthy and very popular with children. High in calcium and vitamins.

Preparation time: 10 mins
Cooking time: 0

2 peaches
225g (8oz) strawberries
60ml (4 tablespoons) apricot juice

15ml (1 tablespoon) honey, or to taste
225g (8oz) creamy fromage frais

To decorate
4 small strawberries

1. Peel the peaches by placing them in a bowl and pouring boiling water over. Set aside for 2 minutes, then plunge into cold water. The skins will peel away easily.
2. Slice peaches and discard stones. Place in the food processor with the strawberries and apricot juice. Process until smooth.
3. Add the honey and fromage frais and process again, for a few seconds, just to blend.
4. Pour mixture into four wine glasses. Chill until ready to serve.
5. Serve, decorating each wine glass with a strawberry.

Speedy Chocolate
Orange Mousse
Serves 4

A rich-tasting, tangy mousse that's made in a flash. Delicious served with fresh or frozen raspberries, or just on its own with wafer biscuits.

Preparation time: 10 mins + chilling time
Cooking time: 0

250ml (9 fl oz) Greek
  strained yoghurt
Grated rind and juice of ½
  orange

30ml (2 tablespoons) dark
  chocolate syrup
50g (2oz) dark chocolate,
  chopped
2 egg whites, size 2

To serve
225g (8oz) raspberries (optional)

1. Put the yoghurt into a large mixing bowl. Gradually stir in the orange rind and juice.
2. Stir in the chocolate syrup, then the chopped chocolate.
3. In a clean bowl, whisk egg whites until stiff. Fold into yoghurt mixture.
4. Pour into a glass dish or into four wine glasses and chill for 10–15 minutes.
5. Serve topped with the raspberries if using.

Easy Fruit Salad

Serves 4

A great family standby which can be varied according to the
fruits in season. High in fibre and vitamin C and quick to put
together, this inexpensive dessert is always popular.

Preparation time: 15 mins
Cooking time: 0

*425g (15oz) can pineapple
  pieces in pineapple juice
150ml (5 fl oz) orange juice
30ml (2 tablespoons) Kirsch,
  optional
50g (2oz) dried apricots,
  quartered
2 apples, cored and diced*

*100g (4oz) raspberries or
  redcurrants, removed
  from stems (frozen will
  do)
1 kiwi fruit, peeled and
  sliced
1 banana or 100g (4oz)
  black seedless grapes*

To serve
Greek yoghurt or whipped cream

1. Turn pineapple into a glass serving bowl with its juice.
   Add orange juice, Kirsch, dried apricots, apples, raspberries or redcurrants and kiwi fruit. Add grapes if using.
2. Toss to mix well. Cover and chill in the refrigerator until
   ready to serve (at least 10 minutes for flavours to mingle).
3. Add banana, if using, just before serving.

Rice Pud with
Fruits of the Forest

Serves 4

A few blackberries and raspberries in the freezer quickly transform an everyday pudding into a special dessert. Store the rice pud in the fridge so that it's served really cold.

Preparation time: 5 mins
Cooking time: 10 mins + cooling time

225g (8oz) Bramley cooking apples

100g (4oz) blackberries (frozen will do)

100g (4oz) raspberries (frozen will do)

75g (3oz) granulated sugar, or to taste

624g (1lb 6oz) can creamed rice pudding

Approx. 100ml (3½ fl oz) crème fraîche (optional)

1. Peel, core and thinly slice Bramley apples and put into a medium saucepan. Add blackberries and raspberries and 25g (1oz) sugar. Pour over 15ml (1 tablespoon) water.
2. Cover the pan with a lid and bring slowly to the boil. Stir then simmer, covered, for about 8 minutes until apple softens.
3. Remove from heat and stir in remaining sugar, to taste, then set aside to cool.
4. When ready to serve, divide the chilled rice pudding between four sundae dishes. Spoon on the fruit mixture and serve, topping each dessert with a teaspoonful of crème fraîche if using.

Autumn Fruits
Amber

Serves 4

Autumn fruits poached in orange juice and served with a quick amber topping – a delicious pud that everyone will love.

Preparation time: 10 mins
Cooking time: 18 mins

150ml (5 fl oz) orange juice
50g (2oz) soft light brown
  sugar
5cm (2 inch) piece cinnamon
  stick

225g (8oz) Cox's apples,
  peeled, cored and sliced
225g (8oz) ripe plums,
  halved and stoned
225g (8oz) blackberries
  (frozen will do)

For the topping
40g (1¹/2oz) butter
100g (4oz) fresh wholemeal
  breadcrumbs
25g (1oz) chopped mixed
  nuts

15ml (1 tablespoon)
  demerara sugar
2.5ml (¹/2 teaspoon) ground
  cinnamon

To serve
whipped cream or fromage frais

1. Put the orange juice into a fairly large saucepan with the sugar and cinnamon stick.
2. Heat gently, stirring continuously, until the sugar melts. Bring to the boil. Remove from heat.
3. Carefully add the apple slices to the pan with the plums and blackberries. Cover with a lid and simmer gently until fruit is tender, about 8–10 minutes. Set aside for at least 5 minutes, or leave to cool completely.

4. Meanwhile, melt the butter in a large frying pan. When butter is foaming, add breadcrumbs and nuts to the pan. Fry, stirring, for approximately 5 minutes until crisp and golden. Remove from heat and stir in the sugar and cinnamon. Allow to stand for 5–10 minutes.

5. Spoon the fruit with some of its juice into four serving dishes. Top evenly with the crisp amber mixture and serve immediately with the whipped cream or fromage frais.

Banana Fritters

Serves 4

Cooked bananas have a very different flavour to fresh. These speedy fritters can be eaten hot or cold, dredged with caster or icing sugar, and are simplicity itself to prepare and cook. They will soon become a firm family favourite.

Preparation time: 10 mins
Cooking time: 2–3 mins for each batch of bananas

50g (2oz) plain flour
15ml (1 tablespoon) rape seed oil

175ml (6 fl oz) evaporated milk
3–4 medium size bananas

For frying
150ml (5 fl oz) sunflower oil

To serve
caster sugar or sifted icing sugar

Greek yoghurt or fromage frais

1. Sieve flour into a mixing bowl. Pour oil into centre of flour then gradually add evaporated milk, beating with a wooden spoon or balloon whisk until a smooth thick batter results.
2. Peel bananas, then cut each in half and then in half again lengthways.
3. Dip bananas in batter to coat well.
4. Heat oil in a shallow frying pan then fry the pieces of banana three or four at a time, turning once, until golden brown on all sides (they cook very quickly in the hot oil).
5. Drain on absorbent kitchen paper and serve warm or cold, sprinkled with sugar and accompanied by Greek yoghurt or fromage frais.

Hot Chocolate
& Cherry Pud
Serves 4–6

This well-flavoured dessert is very morish and popular with just about everyone. Serve either with the hot chocolate sauce on page 140 or with single cream for speed. Any leftovers can be served cold as a cake. You will need a 450g (1lb) loaf tin. Use lard for greasing the tin if possible as this is the best fat for easy release; margarine is also good. Avoid oil.

Preparation time: 10 mins
Cooking time: 40 mins

100g (4oz) margarine (at room temperature)
100g (4oz) caster sugar
75g (3oz) self-raising flour

25g (1oz) cocoa powder
2 eggs, size 2, beaten
50g (2oz) glacé cherries, washed and chopped

1. Pre-heat the oven to 180°C (350°F) gas mark 4.
2. Put the margarine and caster sugar into a large mixing bowl.
3. Sieve flour and cocoa powder together and add to the bowl.
4. Add the beaten eggs.
5. Using either an electric mixer or a wooden spoon, mix to combine, then beat for 1 minute, until mixture is light and fluffy. Add glacé cherries and stir to combine.
6. Turn into prepared tin. Level the surface.
7. Bake in the centre of the oven for approximately 40 minutes, until well risen and crisp and a cocktail stick inserted in the centre comes out clean.
8. Allow to stand in tin for 5 minutes then turn onto serving plate and serve, cut into slices.

Poached Pears with
Speedy Chocolate Fudge Sauce
Serves 4

Ripe pears poached in lemonade and served with a hot rich chocolate sauce – simply delicious. Serve with fromage frais or Greek yoghurt.

Preparation time: 10 mins
Cooking time: 15 mins

4 large ripe pears, peeled
450ml (³/4 pint) lemonade

1 cinnamon stick
4 cloves

For the sauce
75g (3oz) caster sugar
75g (3oz) soft brown
   muscovado sugar
15g (¹/2oz) cornflour

50g (2oz) cocoa powder,
   sieved
300ml (10 fl oz) milk
25g (1oz) butter

1. Cut a small piece from the base of each pear so they stand up easily.
2. Put pears into a pan. Pour over lemonade. Add cinnamon stick and cloves. (Pears should be about half-covered with liquid.)
3. Bring to the boil, cover and simmer for 15 minutes.
4. Meanwhile, prepare the sauce. Put all ingredients for the sauce into a non-stick medium size saucepan.
5. Heat gently, stirring, until sugar dissolves then boil briskly for 2 minutes. Remove from heat.
6. Serve the pears with a little of their juice, topped with the hot chocolate fudge sauce.

Blackcurrant Crumble
Serves 4–6

The fresh flavour of blackcurrants is superb, and with a crumbly topping they become a filling family pud. Serve with custard or ice cream.

Preparation time: 10 mins
Cooking time: 30 mins

450g (1lb) blackcurrants

50g (2oz) soft light brown sugar

For the topping
50g (2oz) plain flour
100g (4oz) quick-cook rolled oats

75g (3oz) butter, cubed
50g (2oz) demerara sugar
50g (2oz) walnuts, chopped

1. Pre-heat the oven to 190°C (375°F) gas mark 5.
2. Remove the currants from their stems and put into a fairly shallow 22.5cm (9 inch) pie dish. Scatter light brown sugar over the top.
3. Prepare the topping. Put flour and oats into the food processor. Add butter. Process until mixture resembles rough breadcrumbs (this takes a few seconds only).
4. Remove blade and fork in sugar and walnuts.
5. Pour topping over fruit.
6. Bake for 30 minutes. Serve immediately.

Spiced Peach Creams
Serves 4

A creamy dessert that's simple to make. Serve well chilled in tall wine glasses.

Preparation time: 10 mins
Cooking time: 0

400g (14oz) can peach slices in natural juice, drained
25g (1oz) ginger in syrup, drained
300ml (10 fl oz) whipping cream, whipped

60ml (4 tablespoons) Alpen No Added Sugar
10ml (2 teaspoons) demerara sugar

To serve
4 fresh strawberries

1. Chop the drained peaches roughly.
2. Fold the ginger into the whipped cream.
3. Layer the peaches, whipped cream and Alpen into four tall, medium size wine glasses, ending with a layer of cream.
4. Chill in the fridge for at least 20 minutes, then sprinkle with the sugar and top each dessert with a strawberry before serving.

Strawberry & Grape Brûlée
Serves 4

If preferred these brûlées can be prepared up to 4 hours in advance and held in the fridge until ready to serve. Pop them under the grill at last minute. Try varying the fruits in this recipe. Pear and peach are good together, so are banana and nectarine.

Preparation time: 10 mins
Cooking time: 5 mins

175g (6oz) seedless black grapes
225g (8oz) strawberries, sliced
150g (5oz) Greek yoghurt

275g (10oz) creamy fromage frais
1.25ml (¼ teaspoon) ground mixed spice
175g (6oz) soft brown sugar

1. Reserve a little of the fruit for decoration then arrange the remainder in the bases of four ramekins or small oven-proof dishes.
2. Mix yoghurt and fromage frais together and spoon evenly over the fruit to cover it completely.
3. Chill in the fridge for 10 minutes.
4. Pre-heat the grill to medium hot. Combine the spice and sugar and sprinkle over the creamy topping.
5. Place under the grill for a few minutes until sugar caramelizes. Serve immediately garnished with the reserved fruits.

Chocolate Orange
& Ginger Trifle
Serves 4

This spicy trifle is a firm favourite with anyone who loves
Jamaican ginger cake. Good enough for entertaining, my
family welcomes it as an alternative to traditional Christmas
pudding.

Preparation time: 15 mins
Cooking time: 0

¹/₂ Jamaican ginger cake,
  about 175g (6oz)
3 large oranges
¹/₂ plain chocolate orange,
  chopped roughly
25g (1oz) stem ginger,
  chopped

300ml (10 fl oz) Greek
  yoghurt
25g (1oz) caster sugar
50g (2oz) toasted flaked
  almonds

1. Cut the ginger cake into 2.5cm (1 inch) cubes and put into
    the base of a trifle dish.
2. Holding the oranges over the bowl so that any drips are
    caught, peel and segment the oranges, discarding all pith,
    membrane, peel and pips. Arrange fruit over cake.
3. Sprinkle over the chopped chocolate orange with the stem
    ginger.
4. Turn the Greek yoghurt into a mixing bowl. Stir in the
    sugar. Pour yoghurt over trifle.
5. Chill in the fridge for at least 20 minutes.
6. Serve the trifle topped with the toasted almonds.

Porridge with
Apricots & Apple
Serves 4

Porridge oats are one of the best sources of soluble fibre.
Perfectly cooked porridge is quick and easy to make and can
be served as breakfast or for a quick snack. This fruity version
makes a good hot family pud. Serve with evaporated milk or
single cream.

Preparation time: 8 mins
Cooking time: 5 mins

*100g (4oz) quick cooking
  porridge oats*
*300ml (10 fl oz)
  semi-skimmed milk*
*20ml (4 teaspoons) demerara
  sugar*

*50g (2oz) dried apricots,
  chopped*
*2 medium size eating apples,
  cored and diced*

1. Put the oats and milk into a medium size, non-stick
   saucepan. Stir in 300ml (10 fl oz) water.
2. Bring to the boil, stirring all the time, then simmer for
   about 5 minutes, stirring occasionally.
3. Remove from the heat and stir in the sugar, then divide
   between four cereal bowls.
4. Top each bowl of hot porridge with the apricots and
   apples. Serve immediately.

Speedy Apple Strudel
Serves 8

One packet of filo pastry will make two strudels, each feeding four people. Freeze the remaining one, once cold, and re-heat from frozen for 30–35 minutes in an oven pre-heated to 190°C (375°F) gas mark 5. Keep any filo pastry you are not using covered with a damp tea towel to prevent it from drying out.

Preparation time: 20 mins
Cooking time: 30–35 mins

*450g (1lb) Bramley cooking
    apples*
*350g (12oz) eating apples
    (Cox's or Worcester's if
    possible)*
Juice of ½ lemon
25g (1oz) sultanas
25g (1oz) raisins
*50g (2oz) dried apricots,
    chopped*

50g (2oz) caster sugar
*10ml (2 teaspoons) mixed
    spice*
*400g (14oz) packet fresh filo
    pastry*
100g (4oz) butter melted or
    85ml (3 fl oz) rape seed oil
*75g (3oz) fresh brown
    breadcrumbs*
75g (3oz) flaked almonds

To serve
sifted icing sugar

1. Pre-heat the oven to 180°C (350°F) gas mark 4.
2. Peel, core and roughly chop the Bramley and Cox's apples.
3. Put them into a mixing bowl. Sprinkle over the lemon juice and toss to coat, then add the sultanas, raisins and apricots. Sprinkle with the sugar and spice.
4. Make first strudel: lay two sheets of filo on a clean tea towel, overlapping slightly in centre, to form a 32.5cm (13 inch) square. Brush all over with melted butter or oil.
5. Top with another two sheets of pastry then brush again

with butter; repeat with another two sheets or until you have used half the sheets in the packet.

6. Sprinkle the last two sheets with half the breadcrumbs.

7. Spoon half the apple mixture evenly over filo, leaving 1.25cm (½ inch) border all round.

8. Using the cloth to help start you off, roll filo up to resemble a Swiss roll.

9. Brush roll with melted butter then sprinkle with half the almonds.

10. Transfer to baking sheet and bake for 30–35 minutes, increasing oven temperature to 200°C (400°F) gas mark 6 for last 5 minutes to encourage filo to brown.

11. Allow to cool for 10 minutes, then serve in slices dusted with a snow of icing sugar.

12. Repeat to make a second filo strudel using remaining ingredients.

Christmas Pie

Serves 4–6

A delicious family cut-and-come-again pud for Christmastime. Serve with custard or cream. Although not strictly necessary, this tart benefits by being chilled in the fridge for 20 minutes after preparation and before baking.

Preparation time: 15 mins
Cooking time: 30 mins

*225g (8oz) puff pastry,
    defrosted if frozen*
*225g (8oz) ready prepared
    mincemeat*
*225g (8oz) Bramley apples,
    peeled, cored and thinly
    sliced*

*40g (1¹/₂oz) glacé cherries,
    chopped*
Beaten egg to glaze
40g (1¹/₂oz) chopped nuts
Icing sugar for dusting

1. Pre-heat the oven to 220°C (425°F) gas mark 7.
2. Roll out pastry to a square, approximately 30 × 30cm (12 × 12 inches). Trim edges straight.
3. Cut in half, lengthways.
4. Fold one half in half, lengthways then using a sharp knife, cut slits through the folded edge to within 2.5cm (1 inch) of the outside edge. Set aside.
5. Place plain piece of pastry on to an ungreased baking tray sprinkled with a little cold water, which will form steam in the oven and help pie to rise.
6. Spread with mincemeat to within 2.5cm (1 inch) of edge.
7. Arrange apple slices evenly on top of mincemeat, then sprinkle cherries over. Brush edge with a little water.
8. Lift latticed piece of pastry onto half of the pie, then open it out to fit bottom layer exactly. Press round edges to seal layers together then knock up and flute edges.
9. Brush all over lightly with beaten egg and sprinkle with nuts.
10. Bake for 25–30 minutes, reducing heat to 180°C (350°F) gas mark 4 after 20 minutes or so if pie is becoming too brown.
11. Serve warm, dusted with icing sugar and cut into slices.

Bakewell Tart

Serves 4–6

A superb teatime treat that originated in Derbyshire, this also makes a delicious dessert that's good enough for entertaining. Serve with single cream, ice cream or creamy fromage frais.

Preparation time: 15 mins
Cooking time: 25–30 mins

225g (8oz) frozen shortcrust pastry, defrosted

For the filling
45ml (3 tablespoons) raspberry jam or lemon curd

4 eggs, size 2

75g (3oz) caster sugar
100g (4oz) butter, melted and cooled
75g (3oz) ground almonds

To decorate
a little sifted icing sugar

4 glacé cherries, halved

1. Pre-heat the oven to 200°C (400°F) gas mark 6.
2. Line a 20cm (8inch) fluted flan ring with the pastry. Prick base and sides all over with a fork.
3. Spread jam or lemon curd evenly over base, warming it a little first if it's very cold. (Warming is not necessary with lemon curd.)
4. Put eggs and sugar into a mixing bowl and beat, using an electric mixer until pale and creamy. Beat in the cooled butter, a little at a time. Fold in the ground almonds.
5. Pour mixture into pastry case. Level surface. Stand tart on baking sheet and bake for 25–30 minutes until well risen, golden and just firm to the touch.

6. Leave tart to cool then remove from flan ring.
7. Serve warm or cold, sprinkled with a little sifted icing sugar, decorated with the glacé cherries.

Apricot & Sultana Loaf

Serves 6–8

Although this takes just over an hour to bake, it is a very quick recipe to prepare and the result is very versatile – serve it warm from the oven as a pud with custard sauce, or cold as a cake either plain or spread with butter or low-fat spread. It's useful for picnics and lunch boxes too. You will need a 1kg (2lb) loaf tin, greased and base lined.

Preparation time: 10 mins
Cooking time: 1¼ hours

275g (10oz) plain flour
10ml (2 teaspoons) ground mixed spice
10ml (2 teaspoons) baking powder
100g (4oz) polyunsaturated margarine
75g (3oz) muscovado light soft brown sugar

75ml (5 tablespoons) apricot jam
2 eggs, size 3, beaten
45ml (3 tablespoons) milk
50g (2oz) sultanas
50g (2oz) glacé cherries, washed and chopped

For the glaze
30ml (2 tablespoons) clear honey

Juice of ½ small orange

1. Pre-heat the oven to 170°C (325°F) gas mark 3.
2. Sift flour, ground spice and baking powder into a bowl. Rub in margarine, until mixture resembles breadcrumbs.
3. Add remaining ingredients.
4. Beat well with a wooden spoon until a soft mixture results. Turn into prepared tin. Level surface.
5. Cook for 1–1¼ hours until risen and golden and a cocktail stick inserted in the centre comes out clean. (If top seems to be getting too brown, cover with a piece of foil.)

6. Heat honey and orange juice together and brush over top of cake. This is easiest done in a cereal bowl and microwaved for 30 seconds–1 minute.
7. Serve warm in slices as a pud or transfer to wire rack and allow to cool before storing in an airtight tin.

Kids in the Kitchen

Barbecued Chicken Drumsticks
Serves 4–6

Chicken soaked in an easy barbecue sauce is then grilled or barbecued until crisp and brown. This is a delicious recipe the kids can help prepare. Serve with jacket potatoes and a salad to make a main meal or just on their own for buffet parties.

Preparation time: 10 mins + 20 mins marinating time
Cooking time: 20 mins

12 chicken drumsticks

For the marinade
45ml (3 tablespoons) rape seed oil
1 clove garlic, crushed (optional)
30ml (2 tablespoons) soy sauce
30ml (2 tablespoons) tomato sauce

15ml (1 tablespoon) lemon juice
10ml (2 teaspoons) Worcestershire sauce
10ml (2 teaspoons) dried mixed herbs

1. Remove skin from chicken by ripping it off using absorbent kitchen paper to help you grip it.
2. In a mixing bowl combine all ingredients for the marinade. Mix well to blend.
3. Lay the chicken out in a single layer in a shallow dish, then pierce each drumstick two or three times with a sharp knife. Brush the basting sauce all over chicken to coat. Set aside for at least 20 minutes or cover with cling film and refrigerate overnight.

4. When ready to cook, pre-heat barbecue or grill then cook drumsticks for approximately 20 minutes, turning frequently. The chicken is cooked when juices run clear when you pierce the flesh with a sharp knife. As you cook, brush a little more marinade over drumsticks if there's any left.

Sweet 'n' Sour
Chicken

Serves 4

Tender, grilled chicken in a sweet and sour sauce with pineapple makes a delicious quick meal. Serve with rice, noodles or just with a mixed salad.

Preparation time: 10 mins + 10 mins marinating time
Cooking time: 20 mins

45ml (3 tablespoons)
  sunflower oil
10ml (2 teaspoons) tomato
  purée
30ml (2 tablespoons) soy
  sauce
8 chicken thighs, skinned
430g (15¹/₂oz) can pineapple
  pieces in natural juice

10ml (2 teaspoons) cornflour
Juice of 1 lime
10ml (2 teaspoons) soft
  brown sugar
4 spring onions, chopped
1 red pepper, seeded and
  sliced

1. Mix together 30ml (2 tablespoons) oil with the tomato purée and 10ml (2 teaspoons) soy sauce. Brush this mixture all over chicken thighs and set aside for 10 minutes.
2. Drain the pineapple pieces and retain. Put the juice into a small bowl. Blend in the cornflour with the lime juice, remaining soy sauce and the sugar.
3. Heat remaining oil in a medium size saucepan. Add onions and red pepper and cook, stirring, over a medium heat for 5 minutes. Stir in juice with blended cornflour and 30ml (2 tablespoons) water. Bring to the boil, stirring. Simmer for 2–3 minutes, stirring, until slightly thickened.

4. Add pineapple pieces and heat through.
5. Cook the chicken under a moderately hot grill for approximately 20 minutes, turning now and again until well browned on all sides and juices run clear when chicken is pierced with a sharp knife.
6. Serve the chicken thighs with the fruity sauce poured over.

Spicy Beans
with Frankfurters
Serves 4–6

A tasty speedy recipe that all kids will love. Serve on wholemeal toast. This snack is delicious with or without the frankfurters.

Preparation time: 10 mins
Cooking time: 10 mins

*397g (14oz) can baked beans
  in tomato sauce
397g (14oz) can curried
  beans
15ml (1 tablespoon) brown
  sauce*

*10ml (2 teaspoons)
  Worcestershire sauce
25g (1oz) sultanas
6 frankfurter sausages*

To serve
wholemeal toast

1. Open both cans of beans and pour them into a large saucepan.
2. Add the brown sauce, Worcestershire sauce and sultanas. Slice each frankfurter into four and add to pan.
3. Heat over a low heat, stirring occasionally until thoroughly hot. This should take about 10 minutes. Meanwhile make the toast.
4. Serve the beans on the hot toast.

Sausage & Onion Pie
Serves 6

A delicious family pie that's easy to prepare and tasty to serve. All the family will love this crispy pie. Serve with a mixed salad. If preferred, prepare filling for pie earlier in the day, adding pastry and baking just before the meal.

Preparation time: 20 mins
Cooking time: 45 mins

15ml (1 tablespoon) sunflower oil
450g (1lb) pork sausages
100g (4oz) smoked sausage (available from the deli)
2 medium onions, peeled and chopped
100g (4oz) button or field mushrooms, sliced
1 green pepper, seeded and chopped

150ml (5 fl oz) double cream
Salt and freshly ground black pepper
15ml (1 tablespoon) tomato purée
5ml (1 teaspoon) dried tarragon
225g (8oz) packet frozen puff pastry, defrosted

To glaze
1 egg, size 3, beaten

1. Pre-heat the oven to 200°C (400°F) gas mark 6.
2. Heat the oil in a frying pan then fry the sausages for 10–12 minutes until golden on all sides.
3. Remove from pan, blot on absorbent kitchen paper, then slice the sausages and put into a 1.2 litre (2 pint) pie dish. Peel and dice the smoked sausage and add to the pie dish.
4. Add the onions, mushrooms and green pepper to the frying pan and cook, stirring now and again for 5 minutes, until onions soften. Remove pan from heat and stir in the

cream, a seasoning of salt and pepper, the tomato purée and the tarragon.

5. Pour cream mixture over sausages.
6. Roll out the puff pastry to fit pie dish and use to top the mixture, dampening edges of dish with a little water first.
7. Trim excess pastry away and use to make leaves to decorate the top of pie.
8. Brush pie lightly with beaten egg. Decorate with pastry leaves and brush these with beaten egg. Make a hole in top of pie to allow steam to escape.
9. Bake in the pre-heated oven for 25–30 minutes until well risen and golden brown.

Sausage Wraps
with Apple Relish

Serves 4

Pork sausages filled with a little mustard then wrapped in bacon and grilled are really tasty served with a tangy apple relish. Kids will love helping to prepare the sausages. Try this one for Bonfire Night or Hallowe'en. Great with jacket potatoes or mash and salad.

Preparation time: 10 mins
Cooking time: 15 mins

3 medium size Bramley apples, peeled, cored and sliced
85ml (3 fl oz) medium sweet cider
15ml (1 tablespoon) white wine vinegar
1 bay leaf
2.5ml (¹/2 teaspoon) mixed spice

50g (2oz) sultanas
25g (1oz) soft light brown sugar
12 large pork sausages (best quality)
Dijon mustard – see method
6 rashers streaky bacon, rinded

1. Make the relish. Put the prepared Bramleys into a medium size saucepan. Add the cider, vinegar, bay leaf, mixed spice, sultanas and sugar.
2. Simmer for 5–10 minutes until apples soften but do not become mushy. Stir two or three times during cooking. Set aside, covered.
3. Meanwhile, pre-heat the grill to medium hot.
4. Split each sausage with a sharp knife, but do not cut right through. Spread each sausage centre with a little mustard to taste. Sandwich sausages back together.

5. Stretch each bacon slice out using the back of a knife and cut in half vertically.
6. Wrap a half bacon slice round each sausage.
7. Grill for 10–15 minutes, turning frequently until well cooked.
8. Serve the sausages with the warm apple relish, removing the bay leaf beforehand.

Beefburgers with
Cream & Tomato Sauce
Serves 4

Nothing beats home-made burgers, pan fried until crisp on the outside and succulent on the inside. Serve with the easy creamy sauce and some stir-fried vegetables for a speedy lunch.

Preparation time: 10 mins
Cooking time: 18 mins

450g (1lb) raw lean minced beef
1 egg, size 3, beaten
25g (1oz) fresh wholemeal breadcrumbs
1 medium onion, peeled and finely chopped
30ml (2 tablespoons) freshly chopped parsley

Salt and freshly ground black pepper
10ml (2 teaspoons) Worcestershire sauce
25g (1oz) butter
15ml (1 tablespoon) olive oil
150ml (5 fl oz) double cream
15ml (1 tablespoon) tomato purée

To garnish
sprigs of coriander

1. In a mixing bowl, mix together the beef, egg, breadcrumbs, onion and parsley. Season with a little salt and pepper, then mix in the Worcestershire sauce.
2. Divide into eight and shape into burgers. It helps if you do this with wet hands.
3. Heat the butter and oil in a large frying pan. When butter foams, add burgers and cook four at a time for 2 minutes each side, then reduce heat and continue cooking for 4–7 minutes, until cooked to your liking.

Remove and keep warm. Continue with remaining burgers. Remove and keep warm.

4. Blend cream with tomato purée. Stir into pan. Season with salt and pepper and heat gently, stirring, until boiling.

5. Serve the burgers with the sauce, garnished with the coriander sprigs.

Iain's Fish Dish
Serves 4

This fish pie has been one of my son's favourites since he was a toddler. Now a keen fisherman, he often brings home freshly caught cod prompting me to make it yet again. Simple enough for the kids to help with, serve for lunch or supper with warmed crusty French bread and a salad or perhaps potatoes and peas. If preferred, defrost fish overnight in the fridge and proceed from step 3 in method. As a speedier alternative to the breadcrumb topping, use 70g (2³/₄oz) packet ready pre-pared croûtons.

Preparation time: 10 mins
Cooking time: 24 mins if using frozen fish

6 × 75g (3oz) frozen cod
  steaks
25g (1oz) cornflour
2.5ml (¹/₂ teaspoon) mustard
  powder
600ml (1 pint) semi-skimmed
  milk

Salt and freshly ground
  black pepper
75g (3oz) mature Cheddar
  cheese, grated
198g (7oz) can tuna in soya
  oil, drained

For the topping
50g (2oz) butter

150g (5oz) fresh brown
  breadcrumbs

1. Defrost the cod. Remove fish from packets and arrange in a single layer in a 2.25 litre (4 pint) casserole dish.
2. Microwave on 100%/FULL power for 3 minutes then turn each portion of fish over and continue to microwave on 40%/SIMMER for 8 minutes. Set aside.
3. Meanwhile, make the sauce. Blend cornflour and mustard powder with a little milk then pour it into a non-stick saucepan. Add remaining milk and a seasoning of salt and

pepper. Bring to the boil, stirring continuously. Simmer until a creamy sauce results (1–2 minutes). Remove from heat and stir in cheese to melt.

4. Using scissors, snip the cod into 2.5cm (1 inch) cubes (discarding skin and bones if fresh cod is used).

5. Put cod into 2.25 litre (4 pint) casserole dish. Flake drained tuna over cod.

6. Pour sauce evenly over fish.

7. Microwave on Power 7/ROAST for 8 minutes.

8. Meanwhile, prepare the topping. Slowly, melt the butter in a large frying pan. Stir in the breadcrumbs and stir to coat with the butter. Cook over a medium heat until crisp and golden (about 8 minutes), stirring frequently.

9. Serve the fish dish with the breadcrumb topping sprinkled over.

Bubble & Squeak Pie

Serves 4

This healthy vegetable 'cake' is fried in a little vegetable oil until crisp and golden. A main meal in itself, so serve with a tossed mixed salad for a super quick lunch or supper. If you have one, use the grating disc on your food processor to grate the vegetables.

Preparation time: 15 mins
Cooking time: 15 mins

30ml (2 tablespoons) sunflower oil
1 medium onion, peeled and grated
350g (12oz) potatoes, peeled and grated

225g (8oz) courgettes, grated
225g (8oz) carrots, grated
30ml (2 tablespoons) freshly chopped mixed herbs
2 eggs, size 3, beaten

*150g (5oz) mature Cheddar
  cheese, grated* or *blue
  cheese, grated*

*Salt and freshly ground
  black pepper*

To serve
mixed salad

1. Heat the oil in a non-stick frying pan, then sauté the onion for 2 minutes.
2. Put the grated potatoes, courgettes and carrots into a sieve. Press down with the back of a tablespoon to squeeze out excess juices, then turn squeezed vegetables into a mixing bowl.
3. Add the herbs, eggs, cheese and a seasoning of salt and pepper. Mix well.
4. Add mixture to onions to cover base of pan evenly.
5. Cover with a lid and cook over a moderate heat for approximately 15 minutes.
6. Pop under a pre-heated grill to brown and crisp top. Serve immediately with salad.

Super Veg Soup

Serves 4

A deliciously filling soup with plenty of taste. An easy starter or lunchtime snack. The parsley radically improves the appearance of the soup. Serve with French bread or granary rolls.

Preparation time: 10 mins
Cooking time: 37 mins

*15ml (1 tablespoon)
sunflower oil
1 large onion, peeled and
chopped
175g (6oz) red split lentils
2 carrots, sliced
2 sticks celery, chopped*

*1 litre (1³/4 pints) vegetable
stock
10ml (2 teaspoons) yeast
extract spread
Salt and freshly ground
black pepper
10ml (2 teaspoons) dried
parsley*

1. Heat oil in a large saucepan. Fry the onion, stirring freqently, for about 7 minutes until softened.
2. Stir in the lentils with the carrots and celery.
3. Gradually stir in the stock and the yeast extract spread. Season with a little salt and pepper.
4. Cover with a lid and simmer for 25–30 minutes.
5. Transfer to food processor or liquidizer and process until smooth. Return to pan. Stir in parsley.
6. Re-heat gently to serve.

Cheese Soup with Herby Dumplings
Serves 4

A filling soup that's high on protein and calcium and originates from Scotland. Children love this slightly different soup.
The recipe is very easy to make so this is an ideal dish to
encourage the youngsters to help with. Serve as a main meal,
with hot baguettes and a tomato salad.

Preparation time: 15 mins
Cooking time: 28 mins

25g (1oz) butter
15ml (1 tablespoon) rape
   seed oil
2 medium size onions,
   peeled and chopped
25g (1oz) wholemeal flour
900ml (1½ pints) chicken
   stock

300ml (10 fl oz) milk
5ml (1 teaspoon) ready
   prepared mustard
75g (3oz) mature Cheddar
   cheese, grated
Salt and freshly ground
   black pepper

For the herby dumplings

*50g (2oz) wholemeal
   self-raising flour*
25g (1oz) shredded beef suet
*5ml (1 teaspoon) dried
   parsley*

*Salt and freshly ground
   black pepper*
30ml (2 tablespoons) milk

To serve
30ml (2 tablespoons) freshly chopped parsley

1. Put butter and oil into a fairly large saucepan or casserole. Heat over medium heat until butter melts.
2. Stir in onions and fry for about 7 minutes, stirring frequently until softened and golden.
3. Stir in flour and continue to cook, stirring for 1 minute.
4. Gradually stir in the stock and milk with the mustard. Bring to the boil stirring constantly. Cover and simmer for 10 minutes.
5. Meanwhile prepare the dumplings. Put a large pan of water on to boil, then put the flour, suet and parsley into a mixing bowl. Season with a little salt and pepper. Add the milk and use to bind dry ingredients together.
6. Divide mixture into eight and roll each portion into a ball.
7. Drop balls into the boiling water. Return to simmer and cook for 10–12 minutes.
8. When dumplings are just cooked, remove soup from the heat.
9. Stir in cheese, gradually, until melted. Taste and adjust seasoning.
10. Remove dumplings using a slotted spoon. Serve the soup topped with the dumplings and sprinkled with the fresh parsley.

Apricot Trifle
Serves 6

This party dessert does not contain alcohol so is particularly welcome with young children who simply don't like the taste of sponges soaked in sherry! It is deliciously fruity so will appeal to adults too.

Preparation time: 10 mins
Cooking time: 0

1 packet trifle sponges, available from supermarkets
396g (14oz) can apricot halves in fruit juice
175g (6oz) seedless grapes (a mixture of black and white if possible)

150ml (5 fl oz) whipping cream
425g (15oz) can dairy custard
4 glacé cherries, halved
15ml (1 tablespoon) toasted flaked almonds

To serve
single cream

1. Cut each trifle sponge in half and cover the base of a serving bowl of approximately 1.4 litre (2½ pint) capacity.
2. Drain the apricots and spoon juice over sponges. Set aside for 10 minutes to allow time to soak in. Top the soaked sponges evenly with the drained apricots. Add the grapes.
3. In a medium mixing bowl, whip cream until floppy, then fold in the can of custard.
4. Spread custard mixture over the fruit to cover evenly.
5. Chill in the fridge for 20 minutes, until set.
6. Serve the trifle decorated with glacé cherries and almonds, accompanied by a jug of single cream.

Apple Sherbet Jelly
Serves 4

A refreshing dessert that's very quick to prepare, but needs to be left to chill overnight in the fridge. Serve with fromage frais or Greek yoghurt.

Preparation time: 10 mins
Cooking time: 10 mins + chilling time

450g (1lb) Bramley apples, peeled, cored and sliced
75g (3oz) caster sugar

142g (5oz) lemon-flavoured jelly tablet
Grated rind and juice of $^1/_2$ lemon

To serve
Greek yoghurt or fromage frais

1. Put the apples into a large saucepan. Add the sugar, then pour over 85ml (3 fl oz) water.
2. Bring to simmering point, stirring once or twice, then cover the pan and simmer for 5–8 minutes, until apples fall to a mush. Remove from heat.
3. Beat apples to a purée then add jelly, cut into cubes with scissors. Stir to dissolve jelly. Stir in lemon rind and juice. Stir in 250ml (8 fl oz) cold water.
4. Pour into 1.2 litre (2 pint) glass dish and allow to cool.
5. Refrigerate until set.
6. Serve the sherbet jelly with Greek yoghurt or fromage frais.

Microwave Syrup
Suet Pud

Serves 4

So simple to mix and quick to cook in the microwave, yet this is one of the lightest puds you'll ever eat. A good one for the kids to help prepare for Father's Day.

Preparation time: 10 mins
Cooking time: 11 mins

Lard for greasing
45ml (3 tablespoons) golden syrup
175g (6oz) self-raising flour
5ml (1 teaspoon) baking powder

75g (3oz) shredded vegetable suet
75g (3oz) caster sugar
2 eggs, size 2
45ml (3 tablespoons) milk

1. Lightly grease a 1.1 litre (2 pint) pudding basin with the lard.
2. Spread the golden syrup over base and sides
3. Sieve the flour and baking powder into a mixing bowl. Mix in suet and sugar.
4. Beat eggs and milk together and stir into dry ingredients to form a soft dough.
5. Pile into prepared basin. Level top.
6. Microwave, uncovered, on 50%/MEDIUM power for 9–11 minutes, until a cocktail stick inserted into the centre comes out clean.
7. Allow to stand for 6 minutes, then turn out and serve in slices, accompanied by a jug of steaming custard.

Speedy Citrus
Sponge Pud
Serves 4

Use the microwave to cook a perfect sponge pud fast! The kids will love the citrus flavours in this one which cooks in less than 7 minutes.

Preparation time: 15 mins
Cooking time: 8 mins

100g (4oz) self-raising flour
5ml (1 teaspoon) baking
  powder
75g (3oz) butter or
  polyunsaturated
  margarine, softened
75g (3oz) caster sugar

2 eggs, size 2, beaten
Finely grated rind of 1
  orange
30ml (2 tablespoons) milk
45ml (3 tablespoons) lemon
  curd

For the lemon sauce
5ml (1 teaspoon) arrowroot
Grated rind of ½ large
  orange
Juice of 1 large orange

45ml (3 tablespoons) lemon
  curd
15ml (1 tablespoon) lemon
  juice

1. Lightly grease a 900ml (1½ pint) pudding basin.
2. Sift the flour and baking powder together into a mixing bowl.
3. Add all remaining pudding ingredients. Beat together using an electric whisk, or a wooden spoon, until light and fluffy (2–3 minutes). Pour into pudding basin.
4. Cover loosely with microwavable cling film.
5. Microwave on 100%/FULL power for 4–7 minutes or until a wooden cocktail stick inserted into the centre comes out clean and pud is well risen and springy to the touch.

6. Leave to stand for 5 minutes.
7. Make the sauce. Blend arrowroot to a smooth paste with 15ml (1 tablespoon) water. Put orange rind and juice and lemon curd into a 600ml (1 pint) jug. Add lemon juice, then add blended arrowroot. Microwave on 100%/FULL power for 1 minute. Stir well. Microwave on 100%/FULL power for a further minute. Stir.
8. Turn pud out onto warmed serving plate.
9. Pour sauce over pud and serve immediately.

Banana Splits
with Toffee Sauce
Serves 4

A yummy dessert with a delicious sauce that's equally good
served hot or cold.

Preparation time: 10 mins
Cooking time: 5 mins

4 medium size ripe bananas   *8 scoops vanilla dairy ice
                                       cream*

For the sauce
25g (1oz) butter   *15ml (1 tablespoon) golden
30ml (2 tablespoons) soft   syrup*
  brown sugar*

1. Make the sauce. Put the butter and sugar into a 1.75 litre
   (3 pint) microwavable bowl. Add the golden syrup (it
   helps if you warm the spoon first by dipping it into hot
   water).
2. Microwave on 100%/FULL power for 1 minute. Mix well
   with a wooden spoon.
3. Return bowl to microwave for 30 seconds on 100%/FULL
   power, until mixture bubbles. Stir and set aside.
4. Peel and split bananas without cutting right through base.
   Arrange in suitable dishes.
5. Add two scoops of ice cream to each banana then top with
   the sauce and serve immediately.

Banana &
Raisin Buns
Makes 18

Bananas are great in cakes. They keep them moist as well as giving a wonderful flavour. These buns are good with a cup of tea or coffee and useful to add to the lunch box too. If you take the margarine from the fridge, weigh it out, put it in the mixing bowl and microwave on DEFROST for 1–1½ minutes for creaming in a flash. You will need 18 fairy cake cases.

Preparation time: 10 mins
Cooking time: 15–20 mins

175g (6oz) polyunsaturated margarine, at room temperature
75g (3oz) light muscovado sugar

2 eggs, size 2, beaten
2 medium size ripe bananas
175g (6oz) self-raising flour
5ml (1 teaspoon) mixed spice
50g (2oz) raisins

1. Pre-heat the oven to 180°C (350°F) gas mark 4.
2. In a mixing bowl, beat the margarine and sugar until light and fluffy using either a wooden spoon or an electric mixer. Gradually beat in the eggs.
3. Mash the bananas with a fork and stir into the mixture.
4. Sieve the flour and spice together. Fold into the mixture, using a metal spoon, until well mixed. Fold in the raisins.
5. Line 18 bun tins with the fairy cake cases.
6. Fill each case with a dessertspoonful of cake mixture.
7. Bake for 15–20 minutes, until well risen, just firm to the touch and golden.
8. Allow to cool on wire rack and when quite cold store in an airtight tin until ready to serve.

Chocolate Cookie Faces

Makes 8

Delicious biscuits that are simple to make. Children will enjoy helping to cut the faces out.

Preparation time: 15–20 mins
Cooking time: 12–15 mins

*100g (4oz) margarine,
  softened*
100g (4oz) caster sugar
1 egg, size 2, beaten

200g (7oz) plain flour
25g (1oz) cocoa
*60ml (4 tablespoons) lemon
  curd*

To serve
sifted icing sugar

1. Pre-heat the oven to 190°C (375°F) gas mark 5.
2. Put margarine into a mixing bowl with the caster sugar. Beat with a wooden spoon until light and fluffy. Gradually beat in egg.
3. Sieve flour and cocoa and stir into creamed mixture to make a firm dough; use hands if preferred – it's easier.
4. Roll out the dough on a lightly floured surface to a thickness of 3mm (⅛ inch).
5. Using a biscuit cutter, stamp out 16 × 7.5cm (3 inch) circles. Re-roll trimmings if necessary.
6. Place half of the circles on a greased baking sheet.
7. Using a small 6mm (¼ inch) cutter (the end of a small piping tube is ideal), stamp out 3 circles from remaining biscuits to represent two eyes and a nose on each circle. Then, with a sharp pointed knife, cut out the mouth. Put onto another baking sheet.

8. Bake the cookies for 12–15 minutes until cooked. Allow to cool for 5 minutes.
9. Spread lemon curd over plain cookies then top each one with face cookie. Dust with icing sugar before serving.

Fruity Chocolate
Cracklets

Makes 12

Always a firm favourite with children, and these have dried apricots added to provide some fibre. You will need 12 paper bun cases.

Preparation time: 10 mins
Cooking time: 10 mins

75g (3oz) plain chocolate, broken into squares
25g (1oz) butter or margarine
30ml (2 tablespoons) golden syrup

75g (3oz) cornflakes or Rice Krispies
75g (3oz) dried apricots, chopped

1. Put chocolate, butter and syrup into a large bowl and allow to melt over a pan of hot water, stirring frequently.
2. Remove pan from heat and stir in cornflakes or Rice Krispies and dried apricots. Continue to stir until well coated.
3. Spoon about 1 dessertspoonful of mixture into each paper case. Set aside until cold and set.

Sherry Truffles
Makes 25

A delicious sweet meat to serve at Christmas or at any time of year with a cup of coffee or tea. You will need 25 sweet paper cases.

Preparation time: 15 mins
Cooking time: 4 mins

100g (4oz) plain chocolate
45ml (3 tablespoons) double cream
100g (4oz) plain cake crumbs
50g (2oz) caster sugar

100g (4oz) ground hazelnuts
2.5ml (1/2 teaspoon) almond essence
15ml (1 tablespoon) medium dry sherry

To coat
50g (2oz) chocolate vermicelli

1. Melt the chocolate in a bowl over a pan of simmering water.
2. Remove from heat and allow chocolate to cool. Stir in the double cream until mixture is smooth.
3. Stir in cake crumbs, sugar, hazelnuts, almond essence and sherry. Mix well, then chill in refrigerator until mixture is firm enough to handle.
4. Roll teaspoons of the mixture into 25 balls.
5. Spread vermicelli on a sheet of greaseproof paper. Toss balls in vermicelli to coat, two or three at a time, then put each truffle into a sweet paper case. Chill again until ready to serve.

Banana Milk Shake
Serves 6

Children love milk shakes, especially if they're served with a bendy straw and a fresh strawberry speared on to the side of the glass.

Preparation time: 10 mins
Cooking time: 0

3 medium size ripe bananas
Juice of 1 lime
50g (2oz) caster sugar
110g (4¹/₂oz) can evaporated milk

45ml (3 tablespoons) vanilla ice cream
300ml (10 fl oz) limeade, chilled

To serve
6 fresh strawberries

1. Slice the peeled bananas and put into a food processor with the juice from the lime, caster sugar, evaporated milk and vanilla ice cream.
2. Process until smooth. Pour into a large jug.
3. Top up with limeade and stir well.
4. Pour into six tumblers and serve immediately, decorating each glass with a strawberry.

Yoghurt Shake
Serves 4

A clean tasting fruity shake that's refreshing after sport. Children will love the rich fruity taste!

Preparation time: 10 mins
Cooking time: 0

2 large ripe pears
150ml (5 fl oz) carton
  banana yoghurt

600ml (1 pint) semi-skimmed
  milk, chilled

1. Peel and core the pears then dice the flesh and put it into the food processor.
2. Add the yoghurt.
3. Add the milk.
4. Process until smooth and frothy (about 12 seconds)
5. Divide between four tumblers and serve immediately with bendy straws, if available.

Naughty but Nice

Easy Peasy
Family Fondue
Serves 4

Older children will love helping to make this easy fondue for a quick lunch or supper for friends. Set the pot over a spirit burner on the table and let everyone dip cubes of bread or crisp fresh vegetables and maybe a few new potatoes, cooked in their skins.

Preparation time: 10 mins
Cooking time: 10 mins

25g (1oz) butter
25g (1oz) plain flour
300ml (10 fl oz) milk
225g (8oz) Gruyère cheese, grated
225g (8oz) herb Edam cheese or Emmenthal cheese, grated

90ml (6 tablespoons) dry cider or dry white wine
Salt and freshly ground black pepper
Freshly grated nutmeg

To serve
1 crusty French loaf, cubed
4 celery sticks, chopped
3 peeled carrots, diced

1/2 cucumber, diced
1 red pepper, seeded and diced

1. In a large non-stick pan or casserole melt the butter, stir in the flour and cook, stirring, for 1 minute. Remove from heat and gradually stir in the milk.
2. Heat, stirring, until boiling, then simmer for 1–2 minutes until a white sauce results. Remove from heat.

3. Stir in the cheeses. Return to a low heat and stir continuously until cheese melts and is completely smooth.
4. Stir in the cider or wine and season to taste with salt and pepper. Add a little grated nutmeg. Set the pan over a spirit burner and serve with the cubed bread and vegetables.

Lemon Flan

Serves 6

A rich pud that makes an ideal finale to a special dinner party or family celebration. Serve with single cream, Greek yoghurt or fromage frais. You will need a 17.5cm (7 inch) loose bottomed cake or springform tin.

Preparation time: 15 mins + chilling time
Cooking time: 2 mins

50g (2oz) butter

150g (5oz) chocolate digestive biscuits, crushed

For the filling
397g (14oz) can sweetened condensed milk, chilled overnight in fridge

Grated rind and juice of 2 lemons
150ml (5 fl oz) Greek yoghurt

1. In a medium pan, melt the butter over a low heat.
2. Stir in biscuit crumbs. Press into base of tin. Chill in fridge.
3. Put the condensed milk into a mixing bowl with the rind and juice from the lemons and the yoghurt. Beat using an electric mixer until light and fluffy.
4. Pour on to cheesecake base and chill until ready to serve (at least 1 hour).
5. Remove from tin and serve, cut into slices.

Tiramisu
Serves 6–8

Suddenly everyone is asking for this very special Italian dessert which, fortunately, is easy to make. Serve it in a trifle bowl or in individual glasses if preferred. If possible make this pud the day before you want to serve it. I have used cream cheese but you could use Mascarpone Italian cream cheese, if preferred.

Preparation time: 20 mins
Cooking time: 0

300g (11oz) full fat cream cheese
4 eggs, size 2, separated
60ml (4 tablespoons) caster sugar
5–10ml (1–2 teaspoons) Camp coffee (or to taste)
100g (4oz) good quality plain chocolate, roughly chopped
5ml (1 teaspoon) coffee granules, dissolved in 120ml (8 tablespoons) hot water
45ml (3 tablespoons) brandy
45ml (3 tablespoons) Tia Maria
200g (7oz) packet sponge fingers

1. Turn the cheese into a large mixing bowl and whisk with the egg yolks until light and fluffy.
2. Gradually beat in the sugar a dessertspoonful at a time.
3. Beat in the Camp coffee until well blended.
4. In a clean bowl, beat the egg whites until stiff, fold them into the cheese mixture. Fold the chocolate pieces lightly into the mixture, reserving 25g (1oz).
5. Mix together the dissolved coffee granules with the brandy and Tia Maria. Dip half the sponge fingers into the coffee mixture, one at a time and use to line the bottom of a bowl. Pour in half the cheese mixture.

6. Dip the remaining fingers in the liquid and place on top of the cheese mixture.
7. Pour remaining cheese mixture evenly over sponge fingers.
8. Top dessert with remaining chocolate. Chill dessert for at least 2 hours, or overnight.

Mars Bar Flan

Serves 6

This chocolaty flan will satisfy the sweetest tooth. Treat it as pure indulgence and enjoy your slice without feeling too guilty. You will need a 19cm (7½ inch) loose bottomed flan tin.

Preparation time: 10 mins + chilling time
Cooking time: 10 mins

150g (5oz) digestive biscuits, crushed
65g (2½oz) butter, melted
2 × 65g (2½oz) Mars bars, sliced

170g (6oz) can cream
225g (8oz) fresh raspberries or strawberries (optional)

1. Mix biscuit crumbs into melted butter and use to line the base and sides of flan tin. Chill in the fridge.
2. Put the Mars bars into a non-stick medium size saucepan. Pour the whey off the cream, then add cream to the pan.
3. Heat gently, stirring constantly, until Mars bars melt. Pour into biscuit base and chill until set (at least 40 minutes).
4. Remove flan from tin and arrange on plate.
5. Serve topped with the fruit, if using.

Lemon Meringue Pie

Serves 6

Lemon meringue pie is simply delicious and very popular. Either use commercially prepared shortcrust pastry or make your own in the food processor.

Preparation time: 15 mins
Cooking time: 40 mins

For the pastry
175g (6oz) plain flour
40g (1¹/₂oz) lard
40g (1¹/₂oz) butter
1 egg yolk, size 2

Cold water to mix or use
   175g (6oz) ready made
   shortcrust pastry

For the filling
Grated rind and juice of 2
   large lemons and 1 lime
45ml (3 tablespoons)
   cornflour

50g (2oz) caster sugar
2 egg yolks, size 2
40g (1¹/₂oz) butter

For the meringue
3 egg whites, size 2

175g (6oz) caster sugar

1. Pre-heat the oven to 190°C (375°F) gas mark 5.
2. Make the pastry using the food processor, following directions in your instruction book.
3. On a lightly floured board, roll out pastry and use to line a 20cm (8 inch) flan tin. Prick over base with a fork.
4. Bake blind on high shelf for 20–25 minutes, or until cooked.
5. As soon as you remove pastry, reduce oven temperature to 180°C (350°F) gas mark 4.
6. Meanwhile, prepare the filling. Put the grated rind and juice from the lemons and the lime into a medium size

saucepan with 275ml (9 fl oz) water. Blend the cornflour to a smooth paste with 25ml (1 fl oz) water, then stir it into the pan with the sugar.

7. Bring to the boil, stirring continuously, then simmer for 1–2 minutes until thickened. Remove from heat.

8. Beat egg yolks, one at a time into the lemon and lime sauce, then the butter. Pour into pastry case.

9. Put the egg whites into a clean bowl and whisk using an electric whisk until stiff. Gradually beat in the sugar a tablespoon at a time until a glossy meringue results.

10. Spread meringue all over filling to cover completely, then make a few swirls with the knife.

11. Return to oven for 15 minutes until meringue is crisp on outside and lovely and marshmallowy inside. Serve warm or cold.

Blackcurrant & Cream
Swiss Roll

Serves 6

There's nothing quite like a freshly baked Swiss roll oozing with jam and cream. A cinch to make as long as you follow the recipe carefully. Serve as a teatime treat or spectacular dessert. You will need a 33 × 23cm (13 × 9 inch) Swiss roll tin, greased and lined.

Preparation time: 20 mins
Cooking time: 10–12 mins

3 eggs, size 3
100g (4oz) caster sugar
100g (4oz) plain flour,
  sieved
Caster sugar for dredging

100g (4oz) blackcurrant jam,
  warmed
150ml (5 fl oz) carton
  double cream, whipped

1. Pre-heat the oven to 180°C (350°F) gas mark 4.
2. Whisk eggs and sugar in a bowl over a pan of hot water, using an electric whisk, until pale, creamy and thick enough to leave a trail of mixture on the surface when you lift the whisks out of the mixture (10–12 minutes).
3. Remove from heat and continue whisking until cool.
4. Gently fold in the flour, half at a time using a metal spoon.
5. Turn into prepared tin. Level surface.
6. Bake for 10–12 minutes, until well risen, golden brown and springy to the touch.
7. Put a sheet of baking parchment over a damp tea towel and dredge with caster sugar. Quickly turn the Swiss roll out on to the sugared paper. Trim edges with a sharp knife and spread evenly with the warmed jam.

8. Using the paper to help you, roll cake up. Place seam side down on wire rack and dredge with caster sugar. Leave until completely cold.
9. Serve the Swiss roll in slices, each slice topped with a blob of whipped cream.

Apple Cake
Serves 6

A sumptuous farmhouse cake flavoured with apples and cider and made with half wholemeal flour for added fibre. A super family cake which is absolutely delicious served with Cheddar cheese. You will need a 20.5cm (8 inch) square cake tin, greased and lined.

Preparation time: 10 mins
Cooking time: 35 mins

100g (4oz) polyunsaturated margarine, softened
100g (4oz) caster sugar
2 eggs, size 2, beaten
75g (3oz) wholemeal self-raising flour
75g (3oz) self-raising flour
45ml (3 tablespoons) medium sweet cider or white wine

50g (2oz) dried apricots, chopped
5ml (1 teaspoon) mixed spice
1 medium Cox's apple, peeled, cored and sliced
1 small Bramley apple, peeled, cored and sliced
10ml (2 teaspoons) demerara sugar

1. Pre-heat the oven to 180°C (350°F) gas mark 4.
2. In a large mixing bowl, put the margarine, sugar, eggs, flours and cider or wine. Beat using an electric mixer until light and fluffy (2–3 minutes).
3. Fold in apricots and mixed spice.
4. Spoon mixture into prepared tin. Level surface.
5. Arrange apple slices in four lines, pressing down gently. Sprinkle with demerara sugar.
6. Bake for 35 minutes, until well risen and firm to the touch. Transfer to wire cooling rack.
7. Allow to cool, then serve cut into squares.

Flapjacks
Makes 12

These are delicious sticky biscuits that have been popular from generation to generation. There is still nothing quite like flapjack. It will be much easier to measure the syrup if you warm the tablespoon first. You will need a 20 × 16 × 4cm deep (8 × 6 × 1½ inch deep) tin. For a variation add 50g (2oz) chopped walnuts to the mixture with the oats.

Preparation time: 15 mins
Cooking time: 25 mins

175g (6oz) butter
75g (3oz) demerara sugar

45ml (3 tablespoons) golden syrup
225g (8oz) porridge oats

1. Pre-heat the oven to 190°C (375°F) gas mark 5.
2. Put the butter into a large saucepan and melt over a low heat. Mix in the sugar and syrup and stir until sugar dissolves. Stir in oats.
3. Pour into a greased tin. Press down lightly.
4. Bake for approximately 25 minutes until golden brown.
5. Leave to stand for 5 minutes, then mark into 12 fingers.
6. Leave in the tin until quite cold before removing.

Rich Scones

Makes approx. 11

Scones made with butter and rolled out thick before baking are delicious for a snack lunch with cheese and pickle, or make a wonderful cream tea with cream and jam. Revive tradition and make this easy recipe which cooks in 15 minutes.

Note: As a variation, make cheese scones. Simply add 5ml (1 teaspoon) mustard powder and 50g (2oz) mature Cheddar cheese, grated, to the mixture at end of step 2 of method, then continue as directed.

Preparation time: 15 mins
Cooking time: 15 mins

225g (8oz) self-raising flour	*50g (2oz) butter*
5ml (1 teaspoon) baking powder	*1 egg, size 3, beaten*
	Approx. 120ml (4 fl oz) milk

1. Pre-heat the oven to 230°C (450°F) gas mark 8 and put baking sheet in oven to heat.
2. Sift flour and baking powder into a bowl. Rub in butter using fingertips until mixture resembles fine breadcrumbs.
3. Add beaten egg and milk and mix to form a soft dough.
4. Knead lightly on a floured board then roll out to a thickness of 18mm (³⁄₄ inch).
5. Cut out scones using a floured cutter.
6. Place onto a **hot** baking sheet and brush tops with milk. Bake for 12–15 minutes.
7. Best served warm or on day of baking.

Shortbread
Serves 6

To Scots, the Hogmanay feast is never complete without freshly baked shortbread and it's very easy to make. Just remember that the butter must be softened before you start and use the heat of your hand to blend the ingredients together.

Preparation time: 10 mins
Cooking time: 25–30 mins

100g (4oz) butter, softened
50g (2oz) caster sugar

175g (6oz) plain flour,
  sieved

To serve
caster sugar

1. Pre-heat the oven to 170°C (325°F) gas mark 3.
2. In a mixing bowl, beat butter and sugar together until creamy.
3. Dredge in the flour, working first with a wooden spoon then with your hands until a pliable dough results. Work paste until it is quite smooth.
4. On a lightly floured surface, roll dough out to a circle about 17.5cm (7 inch) in diameter.
5. Prick all over with a fork then arrange on a lightly greased baking sheet.
6. Bake for 25–30 minutes, until lightly golden.
7. Allow to cool, then serve dredged with caster sugar and cut into triangles.

Easy Cheese Biscuits

Makes 20

These crisp cheesy biscuits are quick and easy to make in the food processor. Decidedly morish and excellent with pre-dinner drinks, they are a good way to use up any blue cheese such as Stilton, Danish Blue, etc. For a change, you could sprinkle half the biscuits with a little grated Parmesan cheese before baking.

Preparation time: 10 mins
Cooking time: 12–15 mins

100g (4oz) butter, cubed
100g (4oz) blue cheese,
  cubed
100g (4oz) self-raising flour

5ml (1 teaspoon) paprika
  pepper
1/2 egg, size 3, beaten
Few sesame seeds

1. Pre-heat the oven to 190°C (375°F) gas mark 5.
2. Put butter, blue cheese, flour and paprika into food processor. Process until a ball of dough is formed (approximately 12 seconds).
3. Roll out on a lightly floured board.
4. Cut into shapes using a small biscuit cutter.
5. Arrange on a baking sheet. Brush with beaten egg and sprinkle each biscuit with a few sesame seeds.
6. Bake in the pre-heated oven for 12–15 minutes, until lightly golden.

PART TWO

Summertime Picnic

Serves 6

Make the most of the weather when the sun shines. Pack up a picnic, take off to the seaside or countryside and enjoy relaxing in the open air.

Menu

Italian Filled Rolls
Smoked Trout Pâté on crackers
Vegetable Sticks with Curry Dip
6 medium size tomatoes
Barbecued Chicken Drumsticks – cook 6 (*see page 155*)
Sausage & Bramley Plait (*see page 108*)

~ • ~

Fresh peaches or nectarines
1 recipe Flapjacks (*see page 198*)

Order

1. Make and bake flapjacks and sausage and Bramley plait early on the day of the picnic or the day before if possible. Marinate chicken drumsticks at the same time.
2. One hour before you want to leave the house, make the smoked trout pâté. Pack into container.
3. Next prepare the vegetable sticks and dip and pack into a large plastic box.
4. Cook the drumsticks and wrap them in foil.
5. Make the Italian rolls and wrap individually in sandwich bags or cling film.
6. Wash tomatoes and put them into a bag. Seal opening.
7. Pack flapjacks and sausage and Bramley plait, cut into slices.

Italian Filled Rolls

Preparation time: 15 mins
Cooking time: 0

2 beef tomatoes
6 large crusty bread rolls
90ml (6 tablespoons)
  reduced calorie
  mayonnaise
225g (8oz) reduced fat
  Cheddar cheese, thinly
  sliced

6 slices smoked ham
4 lettuce leaves
1 red pepper, seeded and
  sliced
6 black olives, stoned and
  sliced

1. Thinly slice tomatoes.
2. Slit bread rolls open and spread both sides with mayonnaise.
3. Fill rolls with sliced tomatoes, cheese, ham, lettuce, red pepper and olives.
4. Press together and wrap individually in sandwich bags or cling film.

Smoked Trout Pâté

Preparation time: 10 mins
Cooking time: 0

225g (8oz) smoked trout
75g (3oz) reduced fat cream
  cheese
30ml (2 tablespoons)
  semi-skimmed milk

30ml (2 tablespoons) freshly
  chopped parsley
Freshly ground black pepper
10ml (2 teaspoons) lemon
  juice

To serve
wholemeal crackers

1. Flake the trout into a food processor, discarding skin and bones.
2. Add cream cheese, milk, parsley, a seasoning of black pepper and the lemon juice. Process until smooth.
3. Spoon into a small plastic box. Cover with a lid and chill until ready to serve.

Vegetable Sticks with Curry Dip

Preparation time: 10 mins
Cooking time: 0

2 carrots   *4 sticks celery*
1 yellow pepper, seeded

For the dip
10ml (2 teaspoons) curry   *90ml (6 tablespoons)*
  paste   *reduced calorie*
2.5ml (¹/₂ teaspoon) ground   *mayonnaise*
  coriander   *45ml (3 tablespoons) Greek*
                                                       yoghurt

1. Cut the carrots, pepper and celery into matchsticks. Pack
   together into a polythene box and refrigerate until ready
   to leave.
2. For the dip, put all ingredients for the dip into a mixing
   bowl. Stir with a wooden spoon until blended. Turn into a
   suitable container, cover and chill until ready to leave.

Family Barbecue

Serves 6

The children will enjoy helping you prepare this barbecue that is fairly varied and will not break the bank either. The summer pudding should be made 1 or 2 days in advance and chilled in the fridge until required.

Menu

Grilled Mini Corn on the Cob
Oriental Chicken
Barbecue Bangers
Baked Potatoes
Marinated Trout
Fruity Salad
Tomato Salad

~ • ~

Summer Pudding with Cream

Order

1. Prepare the summer pudding 1 or 2 days in advance. Leave in fridge until ready to turn out.
2. About 1 hour before the barbecue, prepare marinade for chicken, brush over chicken and set aside. Use remaining marinade to brush over sausages.
3. Prepare marinade for trout. Set fish in marinade and set aside.
4. Light the barbecue at least 1 hour before you want to cook and put a fresh bunch of herbs on the inside corner of the barbecue to fill your garden with a wonderful aroma.

5. Wrap washed, pricked medium size potatoes individually in foil and bake them round the edge of the barbecue. They will take about 50 minutes to cook.
6. Put chicken on barbecue 30 minutes before you want to serve.
7. 20 minutes before you want to serve, wrap each trout in a piece of foil to make a parcel, adding a few fresh herbs to each parcel. Place on barbecue to cook.
8. Cook the sausages for 15 minutes, turning frequently.
9. Cook corn on the cob for 10 minutes, turning and basting frequently.
10. Lastly, prepare and serve salads as foods become ready.
11. Turn out the summer pudding once the first course has been eaten.

Grilled Mini Corn on the Cob

These corn on the cob are readily available from the freezer department of supermarkets. They taste wonderful when cooked on the barbecue.

Preparation time: 5 mins
Cooking time: 11 mins

6 mini corn on the cob
30ml (2 tablespoons) olive
  oil

A little salt and freshly
  ground black pepper

1. Par-boil the cobs in boiling water for 3 minutes. Drain, then insert skewers into the cobs – you should get two cobs onto each skewer.
2. Brush the cobs all over with olive oil and season lightly with salt and pepper.
3. Grill over the hot coals for about 8 minutes, turning once and brushing with a little more olive oil as they cook.

Oriental Chicken

Preparation time: 10 mins + marinating time
Cooking time: 35 mins

6 part-boned chicken breasts   6 shallots
6 thick slices fresh lime   Olive oil for brushing

For the basting sauce
60ml (4 tablespoons)   30ml (2 tablespoons) red
  sunflower oil   wine vinegar
45ml (3 tablespoons) soy   5ml (1 teaspoon) oregano
  sauce   Grated rind of $^1/_2$ lemon
10ml (2 teaspoons) clear   Salt and freshly ground
  honey   black pepper
30ml (2 tablespoons) tomato
  purée

1. In a small bowl blend the sunflower oil with the soy sauce,
   honey, tomato purée, vinegar, oregano and lemon rind.
   Stir in a seasoning of salt and pepper.
2. Arrange the chicken breasts, in a single layer in a shallow
   dish. Brush all over with the basting sauce then cover and
   set aside for at least 30 minutes (or cover with cling film
   and refrigerate overnight).
3. When ready to cook, thread each chicken breast onto a
   metal skewer with 1 slice lime and 1 shallot.
4. Brush with olive oil and cook on barbecue, turning
   frequently for 35 minutes until completely cooked.

Barbecue Bangers

Preparation time: 10 mins + marinating time
Cooking time: 15 mins

*450g (1lb) thin pork
  sausages*
*About 6 rashers rindless
  streaky bacon, halved
  vertically and stretched out
  with back of a knife*

*30ml (2 tablespoons) tomato
  sauce*
1 clove garlic, crushed
*5ml (1 teaspoon)
  Worcestershire sauce*

1. Wrap each sausage in half a slice of streaky bacon.
2. Combine remaining ingredients in a small bowl. Brush all over sausages. Set aside for 15 minutes.
3. Barbecue for approximately 15 minutes, turning frequently until cooked.

Baked Potatoes

Preparation time: 10 mins + marinating time
Cooking time: 50 mins

6 small baking potatoes   Salt
15ml (1 tablespoon) olive oil

To serve
150ml (5 fl oz) soured cream   2 spring onions, chopped
                                 finely

1. Scrub the potatoes clean, then cut a cross in the top of each one with a sharp knife.
2. Brush potatoes all over with olive oil and sprinkle with salt. Wrap each potato individually in foil.
3. Bake the potatoes round the edge of the barbecue for approximately 50 minutes, until tender.
4. Serve the potatoes, pushing each one up from base to open into a waterlily.
5. Offer the bowl of soured cream separately, topped with the spring onions.

Marinated Trout

Preparation time: 5 mins + marinating time
Cooking time: 20–30 mins

6 small rainbow trout,
  cleaned

For the marinade
120ml (4 fl oz) apple juice
60ml (4 tablespoons) olive
  oil
2 cloves garlic, crushed
Grated rind of 1/2 orange

15ml (1 tablespoon) freshly
  snipped basil
5ml (1 teaspoon) granary
  mustard
Freshly ground black pepper

1. Blot the trout dry on absorbent kitchen paper then arrange them in a single layer in a shallow dish. Make a shallow cut in the side of each fish.
2. Combine all the ingredients for the marinade in a small bowl. Whisk with a fork then pour over fish. Refrigerate, covered, for 30 minutes or up to 1 hour.
3. Wrap fish individually in foil to form loose parcels.
4. Cook on the edge of the barbecue for 20–30 minutes. Serve in the parcel.

Fruity Salad

A simple salad that's so quick to prepare.

Preparation time: 15 mins
Cooking time: 0

*1 large bag Continental salad
  leaves (available ready to
  serve at large
  supermarkets)
1 kiwi fruit, peeled and
  sliced*

*1 small ripe avocado, peeled,
  stoned, chopped and
  tossed in 15ml (1
  tablespoon) lemon juice*

For the dressing
*45ml (3 tablespoons) olive
  oil
15ml (1 tablespoon) red wine
  vinegar*

*30ml (2 tablespoons) freshly
  chopped herbs (oregano,
  parsley, thyme, chives)
Grated rind of $^1/_2$ lemon
5ml (1 teaspoon) Dijon
  mustard*

1. Turn the Continental leaves into a salad bowl. Add kiwi fruit and prepared avocado.
2. When ready to serve, put all ingredients for dressing into a screw-top jar. Shake well to form an emulsion.
3. Pour dressing over salad. Toss to coat and serve immediately.

Tomato Salad

Preparation time: 10 mins
Cooking time: 0

350g (12oz) tomatoes, sliced
3 spring onions, chopped
1/2 yellow pepper, seeded and
  chopped

60ml (4 tablespoons)
  reduced fat vinaigrette
15ml (1 tablespoon)
  honey-toasted sunflower
  seeds

1. Arrange tomatoes in a fairly shallow round dish. Add spring onions and yellow pepper. Pour over the vinaigrette.
2. Serve immediately, sprinkled with the sunflower seeds.

Summer Pudding

Preparation time: 15 mins
Cooking time: 5 mins

350g (12oz) raspberries
350g (12oz) redcurrants,
removed from stems
350g (12oz) blackcurrants,
removed from stems

225g (8oz) strawberries,
halved
100g (4oz) muscovado
golden brown sugar
10 slices from a large cut
brown or white loaf

To serve
225g (8oz) strawberries and
raspberries, mixed

300ml (10 fl oz) whipped
cream

1. Put prepared fruits with the sugar into a large saucepan. Heat over a gentle heat, stirring occasionally for 5 minutes.
2. Cool, then drain through a sieve. Reserve juice.
3. Cut crusts from bread then cut a circle of bread to fit the base of a 1.2 litre (2 pint) pudding basin. Cut remaining bread into 2.5cm (1 inch) strips. Dip bread in reserved juice then use to line base and sides of pudding basin, allowing strips to overlap slightly round sides.
4. Spoon fruit into basin. Add remaining reserved juice. Use remaining bread to form a lid.
5. Top with a saucer and a heavy weight such as a can of syrup. Refrigerate overnight.
6. When ready to serve, turn out onto a serving plate and serve surrounded by the sliced strawberries and the raspberries, accompanied by a bowl of whipped cream.

Midsummer's Day Meal

Serves 6

Summer is the time for eating simple food in the open air, so enjoy preparing this easy menu. The dishes have been specially designed so that you will be able to socialize just like everyone else!

Menu

Lemon Roast Chicken
Cracked Wheat Salad
Leaf Salad
Basket of bread rolls and butter or spread

~ ● ~

Easy Berry Pud with Cream

Order

1. Prepare cracked wheat salad, cover and chill in refrigerator. This can be done well in advance.
2. Prepare salad and arrange in bowl, cover and chill in refrigerator. This, too, can be prepared well in advance but don't add the dressing or the croûtons until you are ready to serve.
3. About 1 hour before your guests are due to arrive, prepare the berry pud. Chill in the fridge.
4. Lastly, about 45 minutes before people arrive, prepare and cook the chicken.
5. Once cooked and after standing time, the chicken will wait happily until you wish to carve.

Lemon Roast Chicken

This speedy recipe uses the microwave – a delicious and fast way to cook chicken to perfection.

Preparation time: 10 mins
Cooking time: 30 mins + 20 mins standing

1.75kg (4lb) roasting
*   chicken, fresh if possible*
40g (1¹/₂oz) butter

10–15ml (2–3 teaspoons)
*   chicken seasoning*
5ml (1 teaspoon) dried
*   oregano*

For the stuffing
100g (4oz) fresh wholemeal
*   breadcrumbs*
10ml (2 teaspoons) dried
*   parsley*
Grated rind and juice of ¹/₂
*   lemon*

1 small onion, peeled and
*   finely chopped*
50g (2oz) butter, grated
25g (1oz) walnuts, chopped
Salt and freshly ground
*   black pepper*
1 egg, size 3

1. Prepare the stuffing. In a 1.75 litre (3 pint) bowl, put the breadcrumbs, parsley, rind and juice of the lemon, onion, butter and walnuts.
2. Season with a little salt and pepper, then beat the egg and add. Mix well to combine.
3. Spoon the stuffing into the neck end of the bird. Secure with wooden cocktail sticks then put any remaining stuffing into body cavity.
4. Put the butter into a mug and microwave on 70%/ROAST for about 30 seconds, to melt.
5. Using a pastry brush, brush bird all over with melted butter.
6. Combine chicken seasoning and herbs together and sprinkle all over bird.

7. Weigh prepared chicken and calculate cooking time – allow 7 minutes per 450g (1lb) on 100%/FULL power. Tie legs together firmly with string.
8. Arrange the bird breast side down on an upturned tea plate in a suitable microwave roasting dish.
9. Cover bird with a lid or a split roasting bag.
10. Microwave for half the calculated cooking time. Turn bird over and continue to cook for remaining time.
11. Remove from microwave, cover with a tent of foil and allow to stand for 20 minutes before carving.
12. Should you want a crisp skin, after the standing time, pop the bird into a conventional oven pre-heated to 220°C (425°F) gas mark 7 for 10 minutes or so.

Cracked Wheat Salad

Cracked wheat is rather like rice to eat but it's much easier to deal with as it's pre-cooked. You'll find it in leading supermarkets.

Preparation time: 15 mins
Cooking time: 3 mins + 20 mins standing time

225g (8oz) bulghur wheat
1/2 cucumber
1 red pepper, seeded and
    chopped

326g (11 1/2oz) can sweetcorn
    kernels, drained
45ml (3 tablespoons) freshly
    chopped herbs, basil,
    chives, parsley, marjoram

For the dressing
Grated rind of 1/2 lemon
Juice of 1 lemon
60ml (4 tablespoons) olive
    oil

Salt and freshly ground
    black pepper
1.25ml (1/2 teaspoon) soft
    brown sugar

To serve
50g (2oz) pistachio nuts, chopped or 50g (2oz) toasted
    sunflower seeds

1. Put the bulghur wheat into a mixing bowl and pour over 450ml (15 fl oz) boiling water. Fork through, then cover the bowl with microwave cling film and microwave on 100%/FULL power for 3 minutes. Set aside until cool, stirring with a fork occasionally.
2. Once the bulghur wheat has stood for about 20 minutes, it will swell up and resemble cooked rice. It is now ready to serve, but can also be eaten cold.
3. Dice cucumber and add to the bowl with the red pepper and drained sweetcorn. Add the herbs and toss lightly with a fork to mix ingredients.

4. Prepare the dressing. Put the rind and juice from the lemon into a mug or glass. Add the olive oil and a seasoning of salt and pepper with the sugar. Whisk lightly with a fork and pour over salad. Toss well to coat.

5. Just before serving, sprinkle with the pistachio nuts or sunflower seeds.

Leaf Salad

This summer leaf salad can be put together very quickly; it also works out cheaper than the bags of salad leaves you can buy in the supermarket.

Preparation time: 10 mins
Cooking time: 0

*1 round lettuce, Butterhead
    if possible, well washed
100g (4oz) red cabbage,
    shredded finely*

*Handful basil leaves
1 box mustard and cress
1 orange*

For the dressing
*45ml (3 tablespoons)
    sunflower oil
15ml (1 tablespoon) white
    wine vinegar*

*5ml (1 teaspoon) granary
    mustard
Salt and freshly ground
    black pepper
Grated rind of 1/2 orange*

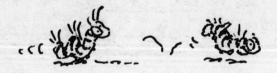

1. Tear the washed lettuce leaves into a salad bowl, discarding outer leaves.
2. Add the red cabbage with the basil. Snip the mustard and cress over the salad.
3. When ready to serve put all ingredients for the dressing into a screw-top jar. Shake well. Pour over salad and toss to coat.
4. Peel and segment orange, discarding pith, membrane and pips. Add to salad and serve immediately.

Easy Berry Pud with Cream

This fruity pudding looks sensational yet takes only minutes to prepare and is popular with everyone. During winter months this recipe works well with frozen berries which defrost fairly rapidly in the flan case.

Preparation time: 8 mins
Cooking time: 5 mins

25cm (10 inch) sponge flan case (available from supermarkets)
38g (1³/₈oz) sachet red coloured jelly glaze mix
25g (1oz) caster sugar

225g (8oz) small strawberries or blackberries
100g (4oz) raspberries
100g (4oz) redcurrants, removed from stem
15ml (1 tablespoon) icing sugar, sieved

To decorate
fresh mint leaves

To serve
whipped cream or Greek yoghurt

1. Arrange the sponge flan case on a flat serving plate.
2. Stir contents of jelly glaze sachet into 200ml (7 fl oz) cold water in a medium saucepan. Stir in the caster sugar.
3. Heat to boiling, stirring continuously. Remove from heat and set aside to cool for 5 minutes or so.
4. Meanwhile arrange fresh fruits in the flan case. Sprinkle with icing sugar.
5. Spoon the jelly glaze evenly over the fruit. Set aside for 10 minutes or so, then decorate with mint leaves and serve with cream or Greek yoghurt.

Birthday Celebration

Serves 12

A selection of cold dishes with a hot main course which is quickly cooked or may be made in advance and re-heated to serve, if preferred.

Menu

Curried Egg Starter (use double the recipe on page 24)
Pork & Red Wine Casserole
Spinach & Cos Salad
French bread

~ ● ~

Chocolate Gateau
Easy Fruit Salad (double the recipe on page 134)
Single cream

Order

1. Well in advance and preferably the day before, prepare the chocolate gateau, which can be frozen and defrosted overnight in fridge if this suits you better.
2. Prepare and chill the curried egg starter on the morning of the party, well in advance. Cover the plate tightly with cling film as hard-boiled eggs have a pungent aroma.
3. About 1½ hours before your guests arrive, prepare the fruit salad, cover and chill in the fridge until ready to serve.
4. Prepare and cook the pork and red wine casserole next.
5. Whilst pork casserole is simmering, prepare the spinach and cos salad, cover and chill until ready to serve. Add the dressing on serving.
6. Don't be tempted to slice the French bread until guests are ready to eat as it dries out very quickly.

Pork & Red Wine Casserole

Preparation time: 20 mins
Cooking time: 40 mins

30ml (2 tablespoons) olive oil

1.75kg (4lb) minced pork

225g (8oz) streaky bacon, rinded

3 large onions, peeled and chopped

225g (8oz) button mushrooms, sliced

3 cloves garlic, crushed

2 × 400g (14oz) cans chopped tomatoes

2 medium Cox's apples, peeled, cored and chopped

300ml (10 fl oz) vegetable stock

300ml (10 fl oz) red wine

30ml (2 tablespoons) tomato purée

60ml (4 tablespoons) freshly chopped parsley

Salt and freshly ground black pepper

2 × 432g (15½oz) cans red kidney beans, drained and rinsed

1. Divide the oil between two large stove top casseroles. Heat.
2. Divide pork, bacon and onions between the casseroles and fry for 10–12 minutes, stirring fairly frequently, until browned.
3. Add mushrooms and garlic to the two casseroles and cook for a further 5 minutes.
4. Stir one can of tomatoes into each casserole. Add one prepared Cox's apple to each casserole with half the stock, wine, tomato purée and parsley. Season with salt and pepper. Bring to the boil.
5. Simmer, covered, for 20 minutes, stirring occasionally.
6. Stir in red kidney beans and heat for 3–4 minutes before serving.

Spinach & Cos Salad

Raw spinach makes a delicious salad and when teamed with cos lettuce and pecan nuts, this crunchy dish is wonderful with the rich casserole.

Preparation time: 15 mins
Cooking time: 0

100g (4oz) young spinach leaves
1 Cos lettuce
1 bunch spring onions

100g (4oz) pecan nuts, chopped
100g (4oz) dried apricots, chopped

For the dressing
180ml (12 tablespoons) olive oil
75ml (5 tablespoons) red wine vinegar
5ml (1 teaspoon) soft brown sugar

5ml (1 teaspoon) mustard powder
Salt and freshly ground black pepper
Grated rind of 1 lemon

1. Wash spinach leaves in several changes of cold water. Remove and discard stems.
2. Wash lettuce leaves, discarding some of the outer ones if necessary.
3. Tear spinach and cos lettuce into pieces and divide between two salad bowls. Add spring onions.
4. When ready to serve, add pecan nuts evenly to the salad bowls with the dried apricots.
5. Make the dressing. Put all ingredients for the dressing into a screw-top jar. Shake to blend and form an emulsion. Divide dressing between salad bowls. Toss to coat and serve immediately.

Chocolate Gateau

Makes 1 × 20cm (8 inch) cake

A large moist chocolate cake that's very easy to prepare and bake and big enough to serve a crowd!

Preparation time: 20 mins
Cooking time: 35 mins

4 eggs, size 2, beaten
225g (8oz) caster sugar
225g (8oz) self-raising flour, sieved
5ml (1 teaspoon) baking powder

5ml (1 teaspoon) ground mixed spice (optional)
175g (6oz) plain chocolate, chopped finely in food processor or grated
250ml (8 fl oz) rape seed oil

For the icing
175g (6oz) butter, softened
40g (1¹/₂oz) cocoa powder, sieved

175g (6oz) icing sugar, sieved
50ml (2 fl oz) single cream or whipping cream

30ml (2 tablespoons) Cointreau or Grand Marnier

150ml (5 fl oz) whipping cream, whipped

To serve
single cream

1. Pre-heat the oven to 170°C (325°F) gas mark 3. Grease and base line 2 × 20cm (8 inch) loose bottomed sandwich tins.
2. Place all ingredients for the cake into a large mixing bowl. Beat well for 1 minute using an electric mixer or a wooden spoon.

3. Divide cake mixture between prepared tins. Level surface.
4. Bake for approximately 35 minutes, until well risen and just firm but springy to the touch.
5. Turn out onto cooling tray and set aside until cold.
6. Prepare the icing. In a large mixing bowl, cream all ingredients for the icing together until light and fluffy.
7. Sprinkle Cointreau over cooled sponges, then put one sponge on a flat surface. Spread 45ml (3 tablespoons) icing evenly over sponge.
8. Spread cream over icing then top with remaining sponge, Cointreau side down.
9. Spread remaining icing all over top and sides of cake.
10. Serve in small slices with a jug of single cream.

Hot Buffet Party

Serves 6

The main part of this menu is cooked together in one large pot, making washing up easy afterwards. The apple and marmalade tart is delicious served warm and may be prepared in the morning if preferred, then held in the fridge and glazed with egg and baked later.

Menu

One Pot Chicken 'n' Rice with Prawns
Dressed Green Salad
French bread or assorted rolls
~ ● ~

Apple & Marmalade Tart with Cream

Order

1. About 1½ hours before your guests arrive, assemble all ingredients for the chicken dish, but leave the prawns in the fridge until required.
2. Next prepare and bake the apple tart.
3. Return to chicken dish, prepare and cook.
4. Whilst chicken dish simmers, prepare salad, adding dressing and croûtons on serving.
5. Serve chicken, slice French bread.
6. Serve tart warm with cream.

One Pot Chicken 'n' Rice with Prawns

Preparation time: 15 mins
Cooking time: 40 mins

750g (1¹/2lb) chicken breast fillet, skinned
30ml (2 tablespoons) olive oil
1 onion, peeled and chopped
1 clove garlic, crushed
1 red pepper, seeded and chopped
1 green pepper, seeded and chopped
2 courgettes, sliced
1 carrot, diced
397g (14oz) can plum tomatoes
30ml (2 tablespoons) tomato purée
600ml (1 pint) chicken stock
300ml (10 fl oz) white wine
10ml (2 teaspoons) dried oregano
10ml (2 teaspoons) dried parsley
10ml (2 teaspoons) paprika
250g (9oz) long grain rice
175g (6oz) peeled prawns, defrosted if frozen

To serve
30ml (2 tablespoons) freshly chopped parsley

1. Cut chicken flesh into 2.5cm (1 inch) cubes. In a large casserole dish, heat the oil. Sauté the chicken for about 7 minutes, until lightly browned. Add the onion, garlic and peppers and cook for 5 minutes, stirring, until softened. Stir in courgettes and carrot. Add tomatoes, tomato purée, stock, wine, oregano, dried parsley, paprika and rice. Bring to the boil, stirring occasionally.
2. Reduce heat, cover with a lid and simmer for 25 minutes until most of the liquid is absorbed and the rice is tender.
3. Stir in the prawns, heat through gently for 5 minutes then serve immediately sprinkled with the fresh parsley.

Green Salad

Preparation time: 5 mins
Cooking time: 0

1 Iceberg or frisee lettuce
1 head chicory
1/2 bunch watercress
4 sticks celery, with leaves
1/2 cucumber

90ml (6 tablespoons) ready
  prepared French dressing
25g (1oz) packet garlic
  croûtons (optional)

1. Tear lettuce into shreds and put into a large salad bowl.
2. Tear chicory leaves roughly and add to bowl.
3. Pick over watercress, discarding long stems and any brown leaves. Add to the bowl.
4. Chop celery and add to bowl with any chopped leaves. Cut cucumber into fairly large dice and add to the bowl.
5. When ready to serve, shake bottle of French dressing well. Pour dressing over salad, toss to coat, then serve sprinkled with the croûtons, if using.

Apple & Marmalade Tart

You will need a 25cm (10 inch) pyrex plate.

Preparation time: 15 mins
Cooking time: 30 mins

350g (12oz) ready prepared
   shortcrust pastry,
   defrosted if frozen
350g (12oz) Bramley apples

30ml (2 tablespoons) thick
   cut marmalade
Grated rind of ¹/₂ orange
50g (2oz) caster sugar
Beaten egg to glaze

To serve
whipped cream

1. Pre-heat the oven to 200°C (400°F) gas mark 6.
2. Knead pastry on lightly floured board, then divide pastry in two and roll first half out to fit plate. Use to line plate.
3. Peel, core and thinly slice apples. Put into a mixing bowl. Add marmalade, orange rind and sugar, reserving about 10ml (2 teaspoons) sugar first to use later for sprinkling. Mix gently with a fork.
4. Cover pastry evenly with filling. Moisten edge with water.
5. Roll second piece of pastry out and use to cover filling. Trim edges with a sharp knife.
6. Press edges together by marking all round tart with prongs of a fork to form a pattern.
7. Using a sharp knife, make about 12 radiating cuts from centre to outside edge. Brush with beaten egg. Sprinkle with reserved sugar. Stand on baking sheet.
8. Bake for approximately 30 minutes, until golden.
9. Serve warm with whipped cream.

Unexpected Supper
Serves 6

In our house there are often times when good friends arrive unexpectedly and are persuaded to stay for a meal. On these occasions it's nice to have ingredients available that can swiftly be made into a reasonable lunch or supper. This menu is one of my favourite standbys. It's uncomplicated, easy and delicious. The baguettes are baked from frozen, in an oven pre-heated to 230°C (450°F) gas mark 8 for 8–10 minutes, until crisp and golden. Allow 1 baguette per person.

Menu

Leek & Ham Bake
Lemon Glazed Carrots (*see page 84*)
– but add 1 extra carrot
Frozen peas
(cook from frozen according
to instructions on pack)
French bread
(use half-baked frozen baguettes
if you have them in the freezer)
~ • ~
Speedy Chocolate Orange Mousse (*see page 133*)
served with Easy Fruit Salad (*see page 134*)

Order

1. As soon as you know visitors are to stay for a meal, prepare the speedy chocolate mousse. Chill in the fridge until ready to serve. Next prepare the easy fruit salad, cover and chill.

2. 30 minutes before you want to eat, prepare the carrots, then the leek and ham bake, remembering to pre-heat the oven for the part-baked baguettes, if using.
3. Cook the carrots and peas so that both will be ready to serve as you put the pasta dish under the grill to brown.

Leek & Ham Bake

You will need one very large or two average size lightly greased ovenproof dishes for this recipe.

Preparation time: 15 mins
Cooking time: 20 mins

6 medium leeks
1 dessertspoon sunflower oil
350g (12oz) wholewheat
   macaroni
75g (3oz) butter or
   margarine
75g (3oz) plain flour
1 litre (1³/4 pints)
   semi-skimmed milk
10ml (2 teaspoons) English
   mustard

225g (8oz) smoked ham,
   diced
Salt and freshly ground
   black pepper
225g (8oz) reduced fat
   Cheddar cheese, grated
60ml (4 tablespoons)
   whipping cream
75g (3oz) fresh wholemeal
   breadcrumbs

1. Slice each leek into 3 or 4 pieces, then wash well and set aside.
2. Bring an extra large pan of water to the boil with sunflower oil added. Add the pasta. Stir. Return to boil and simmer, uncovered, for 15 minutes adding leeks after 8 minutes until just tender. Stir once or twice during cooking to prevent pasta sticking. Drain and turn into prepared dish or dishes.
3. Meanwhile, in a large non-stick saucepan melt the butter. Stir in flour and cook for 1 minute, stirring. Gradually whisk in the milk over a low heat. Turn heat up a little and cook, stirring until sauce boils and thickens.
4. When sauce is cooked, remove from heat. Stir in mustard, ham and a seasoning of salt and pepper. Stir in half the cheese to melt. Stir in cream.

5. Pour sauce over pasta. Toss to coat.
6. Combine remaining cheese and breadcrumbs and sprinkle all over pasta. Place under a hot grill for a few minutes, until golden. Serve immediately.

Teenagers' Supper Treat

Serves 6

Teenagers love pizza and this meaty version is very easy to prepare. Serve the meal buffet-style so that everyone can help themselves to a little of each dish.

Menu

Pizza Bolognese (*see page 112*)
Sausage Wraps with Apple Relish (*see page 162*)
Tikka Turkey (*see page 257*)
Easy Coleslaw
Mixed Salad
~ • ~
Apricot Trifle (*see page 173*)

Order

1. Well in advance, preferably on the morning of an evening party or the evening before a lunchtime bash, prepare the apple relish for the sausage wraps and then prepare the trifle. Cover with cling film and refrigerate, adding the decoration on serving.
2. Two hours before guests arrive, dice turkey and leave to marinate, then prepare the coleslaw, cover and chill. Prepare the mixed salad, cover and chill but do not add dressing until ready to serve.
3. Prepare bolognese pizzas 35 minutes before you want to eat.
4. Once pizzas are in the oven, prepare and cook sausage wraps so that they can be served warm.

Easy Coleslaw

Preparation time: 15 mins
Cooking time: 0

¹/₂ onion
2 carrots, peeled

350g (12oz) white cabbage
75g (3oz) sultanas

For the dressing
75ml (5 tablespoons)
reduced calorie
mayonnaise
Grated rind and juice of ¹/₂
orange

5ml (1 teaspoon) wholegrain
mustard
Salt and freshly ground
black pepper

1. Using the food processor, grate the onion and carrots, then finely shred the cabbage.
2. In a large mixing bowl, prepare the dressing. Combine the mayonnaise with the orange rind and juice and the mustard. Mix well.
3. Add the prepared vegetables to the dressing with the sultanas. Season lightly with the salt and pepper. Toss together to coat.
4. Turn into a serving dish, cover with cling film and chill in the fridge until ready to serve, or serve immediately.

Mixed Salad

Preparation time: 15 mins
Cooking time: 0

1 Iceberg lettuce
2 sticks celery, chopped
1 box mustard and cress
4 ripe tomatoes
1 Cox's apple

10ml (2 teaspoons) lemon juice
100g (4oz) seedless green grapes

For the dressing
60ml (4 tablespoons) olive oil
30ml (2 tablespoons) red wine vinegar
5ml (1 teaspoon) clear honey

10ml (2 teaspoons) dried parsley
5ml (1 teaspoon) wholegrain mustard
Salt and freshly ground black pepper

1. Shred the washed lettuce into a large salad bowl.
2. Add the chopped celery, then snip over the mustard and cress.
3. Chop the tomatoes, discarding central core and add.
4. Core and chop the apple and sprinkle with lemon juice. Add to the bowl. Halve grapes and add to bowl.
5. Make the dressing. Put all the dressing ingredients into a screw-top jar. Shake well. Pour over salad. Toss to coat and serve immediately.

Dinner from the Storecupboard

Serves 6

This is a rather special family type menu extended to serve six. It makes an ideal meal for friends who drop in unexpectedly and you want to invite them to stay for a meal, so most of the ingredients will be in your storecupboard, fridge or freezer.

Menu

Bev's Spaghetti alla Carbonara
Simple Salad
French bread
~ • ~
Banana Splits with Toffee Sauce (*see page 178*)
or
Platter of fresh fruits

Order

1. Prepare the simple salad about 35 minutes before you want to eat, but don't add the dressing until ready to serve. Chill in fridge, covered.
2. Prepare and cook the carbonara 15–20 minutes before you want to eat.
3. Pop the French bread into a moderate pre-heated oven – 180°C (350°F) gas mark 4 – for 10 minutes before serving.
4. Prepare the banana splits between courses, but get all ingredients organized while the pasta dish is under the grill.

Bev's Spaghetti alla Carbonara

Preparation time: 10 mins
Cooking time: 10–12 mins

450g (1lb) spaghetti
5ml (1 teaspoon) sunflower
  oil
40g (1¹/₂oz) butter
2 cloves garlic
175g (6oz) streaky bacon,
  rinded and diced
450ml (15 fl oz) single cream

3 eggs, size 3
3 egg yolks, size 3
30ml (2 tablespoons) freshly
  chopped parsley
50g (2oz) Parmesan cheese,
  grated
Freshly ground black pepper

1. Cook the spaghetti in a large pan with plenty of boiling, salted water and the sunflower oil, according to directions on the packet (10–12 minutes), until tender.
2. Meanwhile, melt the butter in a medium saucepan, then fry whole garlic cloves for 3 minutes. Remove them from the pan using a draining spoon and discard.
3. Add bacon and fry for 5 minutes. Stir in the cream, bring slowly to the boil, cover and remove from heat, but keep warm.
4. Beat eggs and egg yolks together in a bowl with the parsley and grated Parmesan. Season with a little black pepper.
5. Drain spaghetti and turn into a large heated dish. Pour over hot cream mixture. Add bacon. Add egg mixture. Toss everything together to mix well. The heat of the spaghetti and cream will cook the egg.
6. Serve immediately, topped with a little extra freshly ground pepper.

Simple Salad

An everyday salad using fresh herbs and a lemon dressing to liven things up.

Preparation time: 10 mins
Cooking time: 0

$^1/_2$ *Density lettuce, well washed*
2 sticks celery, chopped
$^1/_2$ *cucumber*
$^1/_2$ *bunch watercress*

15ml (1 tablespoon) freshly chopped coriander
15ml (1 tablespoon) freshly chopped chives

For the dressing
45ml (3 tablespoons) olive oil
Grated rind and juice of 1 lemon

5ml (1 teaspoon) clear honey
1 clove garlic, crushed
Salt and freshly ground black pepper

1. Tear the lettuce into pieces and put into a salad bowl. Add the celery.
2. Chop the cucumber and add with the sprigs of watercress, discarding any stems and brown leaves. Add the chopped herbs.
3. Prepare the dressing. Put all the ingredients into a screw-top jar and shake to form an emulsion.
4. Pour dressing over salad. Toss to coat and serve immediately.

A Family Celebration

Serves 6

There are so many occasions within family life that warrant some sort of celebration. It's nice to have one particular menu that's easy to put together and ideal for a birthday, an exam success, grandmother's birthday, welcome home or whatever. This menu should fit the bill and be popular with everyone.

Menu

Turkey en Croûte (*see page 94*)
Pineapple & Gammon Salad
Mushroom Salad
Basket of assorted bread rolls

~ ● ~

Lemon Flan (*see page 189*)
Easy Fruit Salad (*see page 134*)

Order

1. Well in advance, the day before if preferred, make the lemon flan and chill in the fridge.
2. About 1½ hours before the celebration, prepare the easy fruit salad and chill, covered, in the fridge.
3. Next, prepare the mushroom salad and chill until ready to serve.
4. About 1 hour before you want to eat, prepare and cook the turkey en croûte.
5. Whilst the croûte is baking, lay the table, arrange the flan on a serving dish and prepare the pineapple and gammon salad.
6. You may like to warm the bread rolls for 8–10 minutes in the oven, on a shelf below the turkey en croûte.

Pineapple & Gammon Salad

Preparation time: 15 mins
Cooking time: 5–7 mins

225g (8oz) lean gammon
1 Butterhead lettuce, well washed
1/2 cucumber, sliced
6 radishes, sliced

425g (15oz) can pineapple pieces, in natural juice
100g (4oz) fresh beansprouts, well washed

For the dressing
60ml (4 tablespoons) olive oil
15ml (1 tablespoon) white wine vinegar
15ml (1 tablespoon) freshly chopped parsley

2.5ml (1/2 teaspoon) brown sugar
2.5ml (1/2 teaspoon) mustard powder
Salt and freshly ground black pepper

1. Cook the gammon under a pre-heated grill, turning halfway through cooking time, until well done. Set aside until cold, then dice.
2. Tear lettuce leaves roughly and arrange on a large oval platter. Add sliced cucumber and radishes.
3. Drain pineapple and add to platter. Sprinkle beansprouts onto platter.
4. When ready to serve, prepare the dressing. Put all ingredients for the dressing into a small mixing bowl and whisk with a fork to form an emulsion.
5. Serve the salad with the dressing drizzled over, topped with the diced gammon.

Mushroom Salad

Preparation time: 15 mins
Cooking time: 0

175g (6oz) button
  mushrooms
175g (6oz) chestnut
  mushrooms

1 small red pepper
1 small yellow pepper

For the dressing
150ml (5 fl oz) soured cream
Grated rind of ½ lemon
5ml (1 teaspoon) granary
  mustard

Salt and freshly ground
  black pepper

To serve
freshly chopped parsley

1. Slice mushrooms finely.
2. Halve peppers and remove core and seeds, then slice them very thinly.
3. Prepare the dressing. Put the soured cream into a large mixing bowl. Stir in the lemon rind and mustard. Season to taste with a little salt and pepper.
4. Add mushrooms and peppers to the dressing. Toss to coat.
5. Turn salad into a shallow serving dish. Sprinkle with chopped parsley and serve, or cover with cling film and chill in the refrigerator until ready to serve.

Mother's Day Lunch

Serves 4

A very simple menu for Dad and the kids to put together quickly. Mum will love this delicious lunch.

Menu

Easy Mushroom Soup (*see page 39*)
Tikka Turkey
Pitta Bread
Strawberry & Courgette Salad (*see page 77*)
~ • ~
Chocolate Creams

Order

1. At least 1–2 hours before you want to eat or the night before, if preferred, put turkey to marinate in tikka mixture.
2. Light the oven for the turkey 45 minutes before the meal, then prepare the chocolate creams and leave in the fridge until ready to serve.
3. Put turkey in oven 30 minutes before the meal.
4. Prepare strawberry and courgette salad next, cover and chill in the fridge. Prepare the dressing but don't add to the salad until you are ready to eat.
5. Prepare and cook the mushroom soup 15 minutes before the meal.

Tikka Turkey

You may like to serve a bowl of reduced calorie mayonnaise or yoghurt dressing with this spicy turkey dish. Tandoori spice blend is available from supermarkets.

Preparation time: 10 mins
Cooking time: 30 mins

*300ml (10 fl oz) low-fat
  natural yoghurt*
*30ml (2 tablespoons) lemon
  juice*
*15ml (1 tablespoon) tandoori
  spice blend*

*3 fresh turkey breasts, skin
  removed*
*15ml (1 tablespoon)
  sunflower oil*

1. Turn the yoghurt into a large mixing bowl. Stir in the lemon juice with the tandoori spice blend.
2. Cut turkey into fairly large dice and add to the bowl. Stir to coat. Cover the bowl with cling film and chill in the fridge for 1–2 hours or overnight, if preferred.
3. When ready to cook, pre-heat the oven to 220°C (425°F) gas mark 7.
4. Using a draining spoon, lift turkey pieces into a lightly oiled roasting pan. Sprinkle with sunflower oil.
5. Bake in the oven for 30 minutes. Serve immediately.

Pitta Bread

Simply heat four pitta breads under the grill, turning once. Serve immediately.

Chocolate Creams

A wonderful combination of cream and chocolate with a fresh fruit topping.

Preparation time: 10 mins
Cooking time: 0

*150ml (5 fl oz) whipping
    cream*
*200g (7oz) carton fromage
    frais*

*30ml (2 tablespoons) caster
    sugar*
*175g (6oz) dark chocolate
Grated rind of 1 orange*

To decorate
225g (8oz) fresh raspberries

1. Turn the cream into a large mixing bowl and whip, using an electric whisk, until standing in soft peaks. Fold in the fromage frais and the caster sugar.
2. Chop the chocolate in the food processor and fold into the creamy mixture with the orange rind.
3. Divide the mixture between four sundae dishes or ramekins.
4. Top with the fresh raspberries and serve.

Christening Tea

Serves 20

For family parties it's useful to have several tried and tested recipes up your sleeve and to know just how many dishes to actually put on the table for varying numbers of people. This christening tea is quick and easy to prepare and is designed to feed approximately 20 adults. It is assumed that a christening cake has been ordered from a baker.

Menu

Mixed Sandwich Platter
Le Roule Croûtes
Stuffed Eggs

~ ● ~

Raspberry Cream Buns
Walnut Biscuits
Chocolate Crispies

Order

1. The day before the christening make the chocolate crispie bases, icing them on the morning of the party.
2. The day before the christening, make and ice the walnut biscuits. Store in an airtight tin.
3. On the morning of the christening, make the raspberry buns first, filling and icing them up to 3 hours before the tea.
4. Next prepare the stuffed eggs and chill in the fridge, well covered as they smell fairly strong!
5. Next, make the sandwich platter and cover with cling film, until ready to serve.
6. Lastly, prepare the Le Roule croûtes which can be made up to 1 hour before guests arrive.

Mixed Sandwich Platter –
Fishy Triangles
Makes 20

Preparation time: 15 mins
Cooking time: 0

*225g (8oz) smoked mackerel
    fillet*
*10ml (2 teaspoons) lemon
    juice*
*10ml (2 teaspoons) tomato
    purée*

*100g (4oz) reduced fat cream
    cheese*
*6 slices light rye bread or
    pumpernickel*
Butter for spreading

To garnish
seedless grapes   *fresh sprigs dill*

1. Flake the mackerel into the food processor, discarding skin and any bones. Add lemon juice, tomato purée and cream cheese. Process until smooth. Transfer mixture to a piping bag fitted with a large star nozzle.
2. Spread the slices of rye bread lightly with butter and cut out 20 × 4.5cm (1¾ inch) rounds or triangles using a plain or fluted cutter.
3. Pipe the smoked mixture in swirls onto the bread. Garnish each one with a grape and a sprig of dill and serve immediately.

Mixed Sandwich Platter –
Ham & Asparagus Pinwheels
Makes 20

Preparation time: 15 mins
Cooking time: 0

411g (14¹/₂oz) can cut
   asparagus spears, drained
30ml (2 tablespoons)
   mayonnaise
15ml (1 tablespoon) freshly
   chopped parsley
Salt and freshly ground
   black pepper

2 slices brown bread from a
   large thin sliced loaf,
   crusts removed
2 slices white bread from a
   large thin sliced loaf,
   crusts removed
Butter for spreading
4 thin slices smoked cooked
   ham

To garnish
parsley sprigs   *lemon wedges*

1. Turn the asparagus pieces into a mixing bowl and mash
   with a fork. Add mayonnaise and parsley and a seasoning
   of salt and pepper. Stir until well blended.
2. Spread each slice of bread with butter and cover with
   ham. Spread the asparagus mixture over ham.
3. Roll each slice of bread up, like a Swiss roll. Arrange the
   rolls on a plate and cover with cling film. Chill for at least
   2 hours.
4. Remove cling film and cut each roll into thin slices.
   Arrange on a plate and garnish with the parsley sprigs and
   wedges of lemon.

Le Roule Croûtes

Makes 16

Preparation time: 15 mins
Cooking time: 5 mins

1 small French baguette
Olive oil for brushing
1 mini Le Roule herbs and
  garlic

1 mini Le Roule blue cheese
  and mushrooms

To garnish
fresh dill and basil leaves   *lemon wedges*

1. Cut the baguette into 16 slices, brush both sides generously with olive oil and toast lightly under the grill.
2. Cut each mini Le Roule into 8 slices. Top the 16 croûtes with the 16 slices of Le Roule. Garnish with herbs.
3. Serve on a flat plate, decorated with the fresh dill and basil and wedges of lemon.

Stuffed Eggs
Makes 20

Preparation time: 20 mins
Cooking time: 0

10 eggs, size 3, hard-boiled and halved
60ml (4 tablespoons) reduced calorie mayonnaise
10ml (2 teaspoons) medium madras curry powder
50g (2oz) butter, softened
15ml (1 tablespoon) freshly chopped parsley

1. Scoop the yolks out of the hard-boiled eggs and put into a food processor. Process for a few seconds just to chop finely.
2. Add mayonnaise, curry powder and butter to the processor and process again until smooth. Transfer mixture to a piping bag fitted with a large star nozzle.

3. Pipe the mixture into the indents left in the whites (if you don't wish to go to the bother of piping, spoon the mixture in with a teaspoon and rough up with a fork). Arrange eggs on a serving dish.

4. Sprinkle the eggs with the parsley and serve immediately or cover with cling film and chill in fridge until ready to serve.

Raspberry
Cream Buns
Makes 24

Preparation time: 20 mins
Cooking time: 25 mins

For the choux pastry
65g (2½oz) plain flour   *2 eggs, size 3, beaten*
50g (2oz) butter

For the filling
300ml (10 fl oz) double   *30ml (2 tablespoons)*
* cream*   * seedless raspberry jam*

For the chocolate icing
225g (8oz) icing sugar   *30–60ml (2–4 tablespoons)*
15ml (1 tablespoon) cocoa   * very hot water*
* powder*   *15g (½oz) butter*

1. Pre-heat the oven to 200°C (400°F) gas mark 6. Lightly grease two baking sheets.
2. Make the choux paste. Sift the flour onto a dinner plate.
3. Put 150ml (5 fl oz) water and butter into a large pan and heat over a medium heat until the butter melts, then bring quickly to the boil (but not until the butter has completely melted).
4. Remove pan from heat and add the flour all at once.
5. Stir quickly, using a wooden spoon to form a smooth ball of dough which leaves the sides of the pan clean.
6. Gradually beat in the eggs, a little at a time, beating well after each addition to form a glossy dough. Continue until almost all egg has been incorporated and dough still holds its shape.
7. Using a dessertspoon, spoon 24 choux buns on to the baking sheets.

8. Bake for 12–15 minutes until well risen and lightly golden.
9. Reduce oven temperature to 180°C (350°F) gas mark 4 and cook for a further 10 minutes until crisp and golden brown.
10. Make a slit in the side of each bun to allow steam to escape, then leave to cool on a wire rack.
11. Whip the cream until thick, then beat in the raspberry jam until just combined.
12. Pipe or spoon the filling mixture into each choux bun.
13. Make the icing. Sieve the icing sugar with the cocoa into a mixing bowl. Gradually beat in the water, using a wooden spoon to form a glossy icing. Lastly beat in the butter.
14. Dip each choux bun quickly into the icing then put aside until set.
15. Serve each choux bun in a paper fairy cake case.

Walnut Biscuits

Makes approx. 20

Preparation time: 15 mins
Cooking time: 12–15 mins

175g (6oz) butter
50g (2oz) caster sugar
225g (8oz) plain flour,
*   sieved*

45–60ml (3–4 tablespoons)
*   milk*

For the icing
100g (4oz) icing sugar,
*   sieved*
30ml (2 tablespoons) lemon
*   juice*

50g (2oz) walnut pieces,
*   roughly chopped*
50g (2oz) glacé cherries,
*   chopped*

1. Pre-heat the oven to 180°C (350°F) gas mark 4. Grease two baking sheets.
2. In a mixing bowl, cream the butter and sugar together until light and creamy using an electric whisk.
3. Mix in the flour and milk gradually to form a fairly soft dough, still using the mixer but reducing the speed to low.
4. Put the mixture into a piping bag fitted with a 1cm (½ inch) star nozzle. Pipe the mixture into 5cm (2 inch) fingers, spaced well apart, on the baking sheets. Bake for 12–15 minutes, until lightly golden. Transfer to wire racks and allow to cool slightly.
5. To make the icing, blend icing sugar with lemon juice to make a fairly thin icing. Spread over the biscuits. Sprinkle immediately with the walnuts and cherries. Leave to set before serving.

Chocolate Crispies
Makes 8

You may like to double this recipe for the christening, but remember that most people don't eat one of everything. You will need a 20cm (8 inch) tin, lightly greased.

Preparation time: 15 mins
Cooking time: 5 mins

225g (8oz) dairy milk chocolate
100g (4oz) butter, softened

50g (2oz) ratafia biscuits, crushed or 50g (2oz) digestive biscuits, crushed
75g (3oz) cornflakes

For the icing
100g (4oz) reduced fat cream cheese
30ml (2 tablespoons) fromage frais

Grated rind of ¹/₂ lemon
A few drops lemon juice
25g (1oz) icing sugar, sieved
4 glacé cherries, halved

1. Break the chocolate pieces and put in a large mixing bowl. Set the bowl over a pan of hot water and continue to heat until chocolate melts. Stir frequently.
2. Remove bowl from heat and stir in butter to melt.
3. Add biscuits and cornflakes to chocolate. Stir until coated.
4. Spread mixture into tin evenly. Chill in fridge until set (at least 1 hour).
5. Turn out onto chopping board
6. Make the icing. In a mixing bowl, beat cream cheese and fromage frais together until smooth. Fold in lemon rind, juice and sugar. Spread icing evenly over cake.
7. Cut into 8 triangles and decorate each triangle with half a glacé cherry before serving.

Index